BEYOND FREE COFFEE & DONUTS

Marketing Training and Development

Here's How To:
- ✔ Embrace Your Role as Training Marketer
- ✔ Position Your Training for Maximum Appeal
- ✔ Design and Write Marketing Campaigns That Work

D1384997

Sophie Oberstein
With **Jan Alleman**

Ordering information: Books published by ASTD can be ordered by calling 800.628.2783 or 703.683.8100, or via the Website at www.astd.org.

Library of Congress Control Number: 2002112526

ISBN: 1-56286-316-9

Contents

Preface

The objective of this book is not to draw more people into your classroom training program. Or, in contemporary parlance, our objective is not to help you "get butts in seats." Rather, the objective of this book is to use marketing to understand what motivates people and organizations to invest in development and to set the stage to convert that motivation into action. As the title suggests, this isn't quite as simple as offering free food.

In addition, the focus of this book is not just on classroom interventions. We are interested in helping you to promote a wide array of learning opportunities, not all of which require participants to be seated. We are less interested in quantity—or the number of participants who take advantage of your training products and services—than we are in helping you to reach the most appropriate learners for your offerings. Finally, we hope to help you demonstrate that training has organizational value thus turning the tables so that members of your target audience seek you out.

Why Market Your Training?

Imagine what the result would be if your marketing accomplished that objective. Imagine classroom training programs that are always "standing room only." Imagine organizations in which internal trainers don't have to fight for money or resources and where external trainers are barraged with requests for their services. Imagine companies in which top-level managers not only say they want development efforts in their organizations but are willing to back up their commitment with personal participation and resources. Imagine the right people learning the right skills to produce the right business results. *Marketing can make this imaginary state a reality!*

The importance of marketing is clear in many industries outside of training and development. Marketing is a $200 billion business in the United States. It is estimated that the average consumer sees about a million marketing messages per year, or about 3,000 per day. In 2000, Procter & Gamble spent more money promoting its products than it did manufacturing them.

What you can learn from your marketing efforts over the long term can be used to improve not only your marketing but your training and development offerings as well.

What Are the Obstacles to Marketing Training?

Why do training and development professionals so often overlook the critical marketing function? First, many training and development professionals are under the impression that if they do a truly thorough job of assessing needs and developing customized, state-of-the-art programs, they won't need to do any marketing. In essence, they imagine that a good product will sell itself.

In addition, whether you're internal or external to an organization, marketing can be one of your biggest challenges because marketing is not your primary area of expertise. You're a training and development professional, and few professional associations or certificate programs include training on marketing your services.

Then, there's the reality that you have enough to do with designing, delivering, and evaluating training initiatives. Marketing often becomes an afterthought that you're sorry you didn't have time to do properly when programs are poorly attended, when there's a 50 percent dropout rate in your e-learning pilot, when your reference manual is shelved away, or when you lose a customer.

So, how is a training and development professional to fit in the critical task of marketing? How do you uncover what motivates your prospective customers and then use what drives them to convert them into actual customers? The answers to these questions are the focus of *Beyond Free Coffee and Donuts: Marketing Training and Development*. This book will provide you with guidance, tools, and examples that will allow you to continue focusing on your passion—training and development—and, at the same time, get others to share this passion with you.

Who Can Benefit From This Book?

This book is for any individual who needs to promote development opportunities within organizations. It's for

- trainers internal at big or small companies; companies with or without money
- consultants and suppliers external to organizations with training products or services to sell

- those promoting classroom training (which still represents more than 70 percent of all training methodologies being used) or other learning formats
- those promoting a single product or service, a series of products, or the overall concept of development.

The book is divided into three sections:

1. "Beyond Free Coffee and Donuts: Addressing Motivation." The foundation for a successful marketing campaign is uncovering what might prompt people, organizations, and buyers to invest in development. Section one contains ideas of what those motivators might be and suggests ways to find out for sure.
2. "Marketing Nuts and Bolts." To be successful, training professionals need to apply skills used by professionals in the marketing field. This section contains technical and mechanical considerations for writing like a marketer and formatting like a graphic designer.
3. "Marketing in Action." Passionate marketers keep clipping files of marketing materials they've seen and liked. Section three provides case studies of four blended marketing campaigns you can use to start a clipping file of your own.

Two things make this book unique in the land of marketing tomes: its authors. We are two individuals from different fields who took a leap into the unknown to create a book together. One of us—Sophie Oberstein—has worked in the field of training and development for more than a decade. She brings to the book a solid knowledge of the field. As a result, this is a marketing book specifically for trainers. Jan Alleman has 25 years' experience in marketing. Her marketing background gives the book some perspective and examples trainers have not previously had at their disposal.

How Can You Benefit From This Book?

Here are some of the outcomes we hope you'll achieve by putting the ideas in this book to work:

- targeted learners showing up for classes they request
- more buyers in organizations purchasing—and using—your products and services
- greater participant involvement in nonclassroom initiatives, including e-learning or electronic performance support systems
- stakeholders recognizing your department as an integrated, value-added function, and as a resource for information and referrals

- increased response rates from a variety of commonly used marketing techniques, including Websites, previews, and email messages
- senior managers buying into and promoting your initiatives
- repeat business for your external company
- fewer battles for resources
- fewer or no programs canceled.

We hope that by applying the principles in this book that you will achieve these outcomes with your training and development.

Acknowledgments

For all the individuals who made contributions to this book—in the form of ideas, testimonials, or reprints from their own published materials—thank you. We are also grateful to our research and editing assistants: Lily Benavides, Michelle Cadieux, and Denise Connich and to the design team at London Road Design: Anitra Nottinham, Shepherd Brown, Dave Munro II, and Alex Wright.

Sophie also wishes to thank the employees of the City of Redwood City, who provide her with a supportive and enjoyable real-life laboratory for many of the ideas in this book, and the members of her family, especially Jeff, Lily, and Evan, who have supported her emotionally and logistically in the process of creating this book.

Sophie Oberstein and Jan Alleman
January 2003

Section One

Beyond Free Coffee and Donuts:
Addressing Motivation

****

The foundation of a successful marketing campaign is uncovering what prompts people, organizations, and buyers to invest in development. Additionally, trainers often must motivate themselves to perform marketing tasks, which aren't always an apparent part of their job responsibilities.

The chapters in section one all fall under the heading, "Addressing Motivation." It's not enough to simply toss the words "free food" in your marketing campaigns. But, instead of guessing what draws learners to take advantage of your training offerings, you can rely on empirical and anecdotal research for information about how best to motivate members of your target audience. The chapters in section one focus on motivation:

* Chapter 1: Your Own
* Chapter 2: Your Learners'
* Chapter 3: Your Organization's
* Chapter 4: Your Buyers'

You will find that the information in these chapters applies equally to internal and external providers of training products and services. Whether you're on the inside or the outside, begin here to create an effective marketing campaign.

Chapter One

Addressing Motivation: **Your Own**

✳✳✳

 ## A **Quick** Look

Every single one of us is a marketer. We promote ourselves during job interviews. We promote our ideas at meetings. We position our requests of others so that they will do for us what we need or want them to. We put a positive spin on things when they go wrong. So it shouldn't be such a stretch for us to identify ourselves as marketers when we design, deliver, or sell training products or services. Yet many of us are reluctant to take on that role, even though several of the competencies we already possess as trainers make us natural marketers. Do you have what it takes to promote your training services? Is your organization set up to make marketing simple? Assessments and checklists in this chapter will help you find out.

> ### Chapter **Features**
>
> ✳ Exploration of your role in marketing
> ✳ Fourteen marketing competencies and a self-assessment to see which ones you possess
> ✳ A marketing readiness checklist for your organization or external company

You are a marketer whether you know it or not. You can make your ideas or desires sound appealing. You know how to access your audience to determine who might be ready to do what you want or need them to do. You know how, when you absolutely have to, to toot your own horn, to visibly promote yourself. But, many don't understand your role in marketing training and development. "I'm a training and development or OD professional," you might say. "Not a marketer!"

Your Role in Marketing

What is the role of marketing for a training and development professional—whether internal or external? Marketing is the means to make your customers aware of you and to educate them about what you can do and how you can make a difference. Too often, the realization that trainers need to promote their products and services is made when it's too late, after they've tried to install a solution that would make a difference for learners but found out that the learners just didn't know about it.

Has someone who's been exposed to your training products or services ever said anything to you like, "This is such good stuff. It's too bad more people couldn't have heard it."? Comments like these illustrate the fact that training and development professionals must continuously promote their offerings. And, this precept is true regardless of the type of training intervention you are undertaking, be it the pilot of a computer-based training (CBT) learning program, a self-directed workbook, a coordinated mentoring program, or the introduction of a job aid.

So, what exactly is your role in marketing? That differs depending on a variety of factors, the greatest of which is probably whether you are marketing internally or externally.

What Is My Role in Marketing?

The realization that I had a role as marketer hit me like a brick in the middle of an event that I was hosting for our ASTD chapter about eight years ago. I had assembled a panel of experts to talk about partnering, a topic that members had continually requested. I'd managed to find speakers who represented a broad cross-section of industries and of organizational types and sizes to appeal to our members' diverse interests and experiences. I'd enlisted a well-respected chapter member as master of ceremonies, and he did a terrific job eliciting information that was relevant, timely, and useable.

Looking around the room, however, while the program was under way, I felt a sinking feeling in my gut. Only a quarter of the seats were filled. I was embarrassed on behalf of the chapter and for myself in front of these prominent speakers. I'd spent so much time setting this event up—arranging and preparing the speakers, coordinating the facilities, writing the required paragraph for our chapter newsletter—that I hadn't spent enough time sharing the work I'd been doing and helping others get as excited about the event as I was.

Memories of the times participants had said to me, "That was terrific. My boss should have taken it!" or "You should offer that again and do more to publicize it!" flashed through my mind in a rapid montage. But what made me feel really stupid was how obvious a conclusion it was. A trainer needs to be a marketer. Simple!

Former vice president of programming, ASTD's greater Philadelphia chapter

Internals

For internal trainers—those who work for the organization in which the training will be delivered—you not only need to promote training initiatives and programs, but to market development as a concept within your organizations. In addition to making learners throughout your organization aware of the resources you can provide, you must demonstrate how training adds value.

Internal trainers need to market on three levels, as shown in figure 1-1.

Figure 1-1. The three levels of marketing for internals.

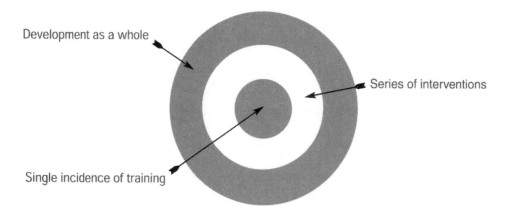

These levels are completely interrelated. Single events or initiatives are less likely to be successful when they are presented in an organization where development is not valued. Each incidence of training is promoted when it is part of a greater series of incidences.

Knowledge of marketing will help you make more employees aware of your services and of how you can, and have, helped the organization meet its goals. This will lead to increased buy-in from senior management, less battling for resources, and more participation in your programs.

What Is My Role in Marketing?

I have become aware of the need to create a marketing plan around each training program I introduce. As an internal, you assume that you don't really need to market. However, folks get a lot more out of the training when they understand the benefits and what's in it for them. Their managers need to have the same understanding. My marketing job entails making sure that all involved understand the benefits of the initiatives I implement.

Meloney J. Sallie-Dosanmu, employee relations and development manager, Just Born

Externals

External trainers—those with products or services to sell—need to develop strong relationships with the appropriate individuals within organizations to demonstrate how their products and services will help meet organizational goals.

External trainers will often, but not always, need to rely on internals to uncover those organizational goals and to promote development as a concept in organizations. Externals will have an easier job of marketing to a company where training is a proven value-added function. The role of an external marketer of training products and services is on two levels, as shown in figure 1-2.

Figure 1-2. The two levels of marketing for externals.

My work	**Myself**
(Product / Service)	**(Relationship)**

Your service can be top-notch and just what the company needs, but if you're not making a strong positive connection with potential clients, you won't get the business. Similarly, you can be well-liked and brought back for several proposal meetings, but if your product or service doesn't meet a business need, you won't land the client. You have the added task of establishing your credibility and value to an organization that doesn't know you.

Externals' challenges are increasing as companies are spending less on outside training consultants and more on wages and salaries for training staff (Van Buren, 2001). You also have a smaller piece of the pie to compete for and plenty of good firms to compete against. Yet, according to *Training* magazine's "2001 Industry Report" (Galvin, 2001), the training industry remains a viable market, with the total dollars budgeted for formal training at U.S. organizations at $56.8 billion. Of that sum, $19.3 billion went to outside providers of training products and services.

Knowledge of marketing is going to make you a better prospect as an external consultant because if you can help the internal practitioner position the training function for visibility, and if you can help with suggestions of how to market the services you are trying to sell, you will have a great advantage over your competitors.

What Is My Role in Marketing?

In this time of economic downturn, I have often been asked how I manage to keep a very full executive coaching and OD practice. The answer to this question was elusive to me—at least initially—because I jumped to the conclusion that I don't do any marketing! I have managed to keep a thriving practice doing some things that I never considered as marketing until I actually sat down and thought about how my new clients find me. Basically, the vast majority of clients are introduced to me through referrals from other former clients. And, the techniques I use to help my current or past clients refer me to their friends and colleagues are actually rather fun and creative, things like calling people on their birthdays, working for nonprofit organizations at reduced rates, introducing my colleagues to each other, and following my passions. So, I guess not only do I do marketing—I also enjoy it!

Caryn Siegel, president, cjs Consulting

Marketing Competencies

Whether you are internal or external, the competencies you'll need for marketing your training are basically the same. Do you have what it takes to be a marketer of your products, services, and initiatives? What skills are required?

Table 1-1 lists some competencies that you'll need, but many of them go beyond marketing. In large part, the skills listed are the same ones you need as a training and development professional. Some competencies are the same whether you're training or marketing, but they are applied differently. For example, a trainer would use knowledge of graphic design principles to create a flipchart for a classroom presentation whereas a trainer who is marketing the class might use it to create a snazzy marketing brochure.

Table 1-1. Marketing competencies necessary for trainers.

Competency	Questions to Ask Yourself
Relationship building	• Do you have a seat at the table when strategic initiatives are discussed? • Are you brought in during the request for proposal (RFP) stage? • Do you have strong relationships with the "powers that be," as well as the target audience for your products or service? • Are you a trusted professional resource?
Comprehension of organizational and individual behavior	• Can you anticipate how people and organizations will respond to your proposals and programs? • Do you know how to assess organizational needs and to determine how organizational culture and events will affect your offerings?
Knowledge of your audience	• Have your programs been designed with your target audience in mind? • Do your materials speak to the learners in their language at their level?
Knowledge of your specific topic or field	• Are you an expert, or do you have subject matter experts on the topic with whom you are closely aligned? • Do you have information that others don't already have?
Creativity	• Can you think of solutions to problems that are beyond the tried and true? • Can you be both concrete and abstract? • Do you come up with new perspectives and creative ideas?
Intellectual versatility	• Would you be ready at any time to shift gears from analysis to promotion, from project planning to designing a training activity? • Do you manage multiple projects?
Cost-benefit analysis	• Can you point out tangible and intangible ways that training is contributing to the organization? • Can you make decisions, for example, about whether to cancel or postpone an intervention, based on a simple cost-benefit analysis?
Analysis	• Can you uncover organizational or individual needs and motivations? • Can you look at complex data to determine trends? • Can you create qualitative and quantitative studies?
Questioning technique	• Do you ask questions that get at the information you need? • Are you an impartial, nonevaluative questioner?
Project planning	• Have you managed all phases of the curriculum design process? • Do you run effective planning meetings? • Are you detail-oriented but also able to see the big picture?
Maintenance and evaluation	• Do you know how to measure your effectiveness? • Are you expert at giving and receiving feedback? • Can you "turn on a dime" in response to evaluation data?

(continued on next page)

Table 1-1. Marketing competencies necessary for trainers (continued).

Competency	Questions to Ask Yourself
Written and verbal presentation	• Are you a brilliant writer—or at least a clear and effective one? • Are your presentations, whether for a crowd or for the individual in charge, compelling and dynamic?
Graphic design	• Do you have a basic feel for how a page of copy should be laid out? • Do you know which design techniques appeal to different types of readers? • Can you look at graphic designs with a critical eye?
Computer proficiency	• Can you use a graphic design program, e.g., Adobe Photoshop, Quark, Publisher, or Adobe? • Can you use multimedia technology to create a cutting-edge presentation? • Do you surf the Web, or use email and newsgroups, to mine the latest research?

As you go through the chapters in this book, you'll see that each is dedicated to one or more of these marketing competencies. The competencies that won't be covered in *Beyond Free Coffee and Donuts* are knowledge of your particular topic or field and computer proficiency.

What Is My Role in Marketing

After two years building my own business, I noticed a couple of competitors who were really thriving with six-figure incomes. They were less experienced than I and not necessarily the best professionals, but they were great sales people and self-promoters. Initially I felt resentful, but then I decided, "If you can't beat 'em, join 'em."

So, I drew up a list of the top 20 marketing activities that I thought would attract the caliber of clients I wanted, including public speaking, writing a column, attending networking groups, and serving on boards of various organizations. I hired a coach myself so that I wouldn't let the 20 areas slip. The result? I'm on track to meet my income goals for 2002.

Jo Miller, executive coach and trainer, Results Life Coaching

Assessing Your Marketing Competencies

So, how do you rate on the marketing competencies described? Take this nine-question assessment to find out. You'll need a separate piece of paper to write your answers on. You'll have a chance to evaluate your performance afterward.

1. List up to six benefits of a pencil.
2. List six factors to consider in a cost-benefit analysis of whether to bring in a supplier to provide computer instruction. (Yes, externals, you do this, too.)

3. Are the four questions listed below fine as they are? If not, why not?

    • On an evaluation form: Why did you enroll in this self-directed learning program?
    • At a client meeting: What's your budget for this project?
    • On the telephone with the manager of someone who has just registered for a workshop: What do you want Madhu to be able to do when he returns from this program?
    • At a design meeting: Will participants be mandated to attend?

4. Name six things that could be improved about the design of the flier shown in figure 1-3, which is introducing a university to the City of Westminster (whose unofficial logo is the cow [C.O.W.]). Concentrate on the graphic elements only, not the text.

5. Rewrite this brief message to appeal to each of the groups listed below: "Exceptional customer service is good for customers, for the organization, and for you! Come find out how at our May 30 workshop."

    • Message to employee/participant audience:
    • Message to participants' supervisors:
    • Message to senior management:

Figure 1-3. How can you improve upon this flier?

COW.University Open House
in the
Multipurpose Room (lower level)

Thursday, January 24, 2002
3:00 PM until 4:00 PM
OR
Friday, February 1, 2002
10:00 AM until 11:00 AM

6. Pull out the last project plan you wrote. (If you don't have one, move on to question 7.) Then, check the box to the left if it contains the following:

    ☐ Tasks listed in sequential order
    ☐ Dates (or timeframes) for each task
    ☐ Reasonable timeframes
    ☐ An advance reminder to those individuals who will have to perform a task in less than 24 hours so they can clear their calendars
    ☐ A person responsible for each task
    ☐ More than one round of reviews
    ☐ A comprehensive set of reviewers (e.g., senior management, legal department, target audience, subject matter experts)
    ☐ Marketing tasks and considerations
    ☐ A task to evaluate or debrief the project

7. Complete the appropriate checklist:

Internals, check off as many as apply:	Externals, check off as many as apply:
☐ I have good relationships with a few key players in each of the departments I serve. ☐ I can get a one-on-one meeting with at least one senior level person at a moment's notice. ☐ I have a champion in the organization. ☐ I have a mentor in the organization. ☐ I have a friend in the organization. ☐ My relationships reflect a healthy balance of professionalism and friendliness.	☐ I have two repeat clients. ☐ I have two colleagues I respect who do similar work. ☐ I can put together a solid project team quickly. ☐ I am active in at least one professional association. ☐ My relationships reflect a healthy balance of professionalism and friendliness. ☐ I am able to connect on a personal level with people I haven't met before.

8. Check off as many of the following as apply:

    ☐ I have studied psychology, human behavior, or both.
    ☐ I read (or at least skim) business books regularly.
    ☐ I read industry journals.
    ☐ I have an advanced degree (master's degree or higher).

☐ I have more than eight years of experience.

☐ I am an avid reader.

☐ I can "read" people.

☐ I know my personality preferences and work hard to understand and to
be understood by other people.

9. Rate your proficiency on the following computer functions using this scale
(0 = none; 1 = fair; 2 = good; 3 = exceptional):

Computer Competency	Proficiency Rating (0–4)
Word-processing programs (e.g., Microsoft Word, Corel WordPerfect)	
Graphic design programs (e.g., Adobe PageMaker, QuarkXPress)	
Presentation programs (e.g., Microsoft PowerPoint)	
Internet use	

* * *

So, how'd you do? Evaluate your marketing competency against these criteria:

1. List up to six benefits of a pencil.

   This question relates to your ability to distinguish features from benefits, which
is part of a few marketing competencies, including written and verbal presentation.
Look through your list to see that each item included is actually a benefit and not
a feature. A feature is a quality of the pencil that is the same for anyone who uses it,
for example, the eraser or the lead it holds. A benefit is how the user gains some
advantage because of the features. Did you have anything like these?

   ☐ It has an eraser (feature), so if you make a mistake, you can wipe it away
   (benefit).

   ☐ It has lead in it (feature), so you can give it to your children if you don't
   trust them with ink (benefit).

   ☐ It fits in your hand (feature), so you can fidget with it in a boring
   meeting (benefit).

   ☐ It's long and thin (feature), so you can use it to hold your hair up (benefit).

   ☐ Its octagonal cross-section (feature) keeps it from slipping (benefit).

Give yourself two points for each benefit you listed.

2. List six factors in a cost-benefit analysis of whether to bring in a supplier to provide computer instruction.

    This question addresses the cost-benefit analysis competency. Did you have anything like these?

    - ☐ Opportunity costs: What else could your staff be doing with this time?
    - ☐ Faster, bigger, better: A supplier may have subject matter knowledge that is easy to transfer.
    - ☐ Timing: Will the supplier be ready to deliver the training faster?
    - ☐ Proficiency: Does the supplier have off-the-shelf or prepackaged knowledge?
    - ☐ Interpersonal issues: Are the lessons more likely to be learned when imparted by an outsider?
    - ☐ Budget: Can you get the funding for a specific external contact easier than you can increase the training or information technology staff budget?
    - ☐ Learning curve: Does your staff have the expertise?
    - ☐ Other issues might include style/fit, quality, content, customer service, economies of scale, and instructional soundness.

    Give yourself two points for each factor you listed.

3. Are these four questions fine as they are? If not, why not?

    This item addresses the questioning technique competency. Did you have anything like this?

    - On an evaluation form: Why did you enroll in this self-directed learning program?

    The main problem with this question is that it is being asked at the end of the intervention. After the fact, the participant's reaction is colored by what he or she just experienced and may not reflect the true motivation for enrolling in the program originally. This is a good question for before the program begins. A question such as "Were your expectations met?" is more suitable following the program. Give yourself two points if you said this question was OK; four points if you raised some like concerns.

    - At a client meeting: What's your budget for this project?

    This question could be a real trap. Potential clients may feel put on the spot. They may be looking for you to tell them the cost. They may believe that you are looking to base your entire relationship on finances. They might be forced into unreal expectations of what can be accomplished in one project if they are forced in to negotiating prices too soon. Give yourself four points if you identified some of these issues.

- On the telephone with the manager of someone who has just registered for a workshop: What do you want Madhu to be able to do when he returns from this program?

This question and its delivery are relatively fine. Give yourself four points if you left this question alone.

- At a design meeting: Will participants be mandated to attend?

As long as it is followed up by questions about why participants will be mandated, this question is fine as it is. Give yourself two points if you said it was OK; four points if you had any reservations about this close-ended question

4. Name six things that could be improved about the design of this flier.

This question addresses your competency with graphic design principles. Did you have anything like figure 1-4?

In reality, this redesign involves only about eight changes. Did you suggest any of them?

- ☐ Deleted multiple cow images
- ☐ Enlarged the cow image
- ☐ Changed the orientation of the page
- ☐ Made the title larger and more centered
- ☐ Put a border around the whole thing
- ☐ Put a few key words in bold text
- ☐ Used all caps or no caps for certain words
- ☐ Changed the font

Give yourself two points for each change you suggested.

5. Rewrite this brief message to appeal to each of the groups described: "Exceptional customer service is good for customers, for the organization, and for you! Come find out how at our May 30 workshop."

Your competency with written presentation and knowledge of audience are being measured here. Did you come up with anything like these rewrites?

- *Message to employee/participant audience:* When customers are happy, they are less likely to enter into conflict with you and more likely to leave

Figure 1-4. The new, improved C.O.W. University flier.

satisfied, which reflects well on you. Find out how to make customers happy at our May 30 workshop.

- *Message to participants' supervisors:* How often are you called in to resolve a volatile situation between a customer and one of your employees? Save yourself the stress and time of this constant conflict resolution. Send your employees to customer service training on May 30.

- *Message to senior management:* Building strong relationships is at the heart of our business. Exceptional customer service is critical to win loyal customers. To provide employees exceptional customer service skills, we are offering a one-day workshop on May 30.

If your messages are specifically targeted to the audience described, give yourself four points each.

6. Here, you reviewed a recent project plan to see if it contained certain key items. Give yourself one point for each checked item in this assessment of your project planning competency.

7. This item asked you about certain attributes of your client relationships. Give yourself one point for each checked item in this assessment of your comprehension of organizational and individual knowledge and relationship-building competencies.

8. This checklist covered an assortment of your personal and professional competencies. For example, it's proven that readers are better writers, so being an avid reader helps you with your written presentation. If you read industry journals, you stay current in your field or topic of interest. Give yourself one point for each item you checked off.

9. This item addressed your computer competencies. You've already assigned your own points for this measure of your computer proficiency. Just total them up.

What Is My Role in Marketing?

On the first day I attended a professional train-the-trainer workshop, my trainer began one discussion by asking an interesting question: "With whom must you compete for your learners' attention?" He went on to say that, when a trainer is in the front of a classroom, he or she is competing with most everyone, including companies like Coca-Cola, who vie for the learners' attention. I didn't like that idea because I just wanted to be a trainer, and I didn't want to be in competition.

Now, after more than 10 years as a professional trainer I realize that every day I am selling ideas to my learners when I'm leading a seminar. In fact, I begin selling long before I get to the actual training because I am advertising my programs, products, and experiences before I ever actually see a participant. I learned that I was my own brand and that to be successful I had to promote the ongoing programs and products of my brand. No matter what my function in training, I learned that to be successful, the most important part of my job was to find and sell solutions to problems that are influencing the organization's bottom line.

Warren Linger, consultant, World Class Training and Linger Research International

Now add up your overall score. The highest possible score is 99. However, your total does not really matter; what's important is how you rate in the different competency areas. Write your scores for the questions listed in column A in the space provided in column B and add them up. Column C tells you how many points in total are possible for that competency area (column E). Column D lets you compare your score to the highest possible score. (Note: For you math whizzes who are trying to get column C to add up to 99, you will be unable to because multiple competencies are addressed in a single test item.) How do you score?

A	B	C	D	E
Question #	Your scores	Highest possible score in this area	Is the gap between your score and the highest score: ••• = huge • = moderate 0 = nonexistent	Competency
7		6		Relationship building
5, 8		20		Comprehension of organizational and individual behavior
5, 7, 8		26		Knowledge of your audience
8		8		Knowledge of your specific topic or field
1, 4, 5		36		Creativity
1, 4, 8		32		Intellectual versatility
2		12		Cost-benefit analysis
2, 5, 8		32		Analysis
3		16		Questioning technique
2, 6		21		Project planning
6		9		Maintenance and evaluation
1, 5, 8		32		Written and verbal presentation
4		12		Graphic design
9		12		Computer proficiency

Just as marketing competencies are similar whether you are marketing internally or externally, marketing techniques are similar regardless of other variables, including whether you're promoting traditional or nontraditional learning formats. A 2001 study by ASTD and the MASIE Center at 16 U.S. companies on the implementation of e-learning, for example, showed that the success of an e-learning intervention is tied to using a marketing strategy that includes face-to-face contact, brochures, and senior management support—the same techniques that one might use to promote any other type of training initiative.

So, the marketing concepts in this book are equally applicable whether you're marketing classroom interventions, CBT, on-the-job programs, or any other training format. The study by ASTD and the MASIE Center summed it up this way: "Just as online retailers are now realizing that traditional marketing methods (catalogs, for example) are necessary and effective in building their customer base, so managers [who wish to market e-learning or alternative training formats] must not abandon the traditional classroom marketing methods."

Is Your Organization Ready?

Even a stellar marketer will flounder in an environment unreceptive to his or her purposes. To market, you need an infrastructure to support you, including resources, a set of skills, and a culture that won't squash your passion but will help you to share it. In this section are provided an organizational audit for training marketers internal to organizations (tables 1-2 and 1-3) and an organizational checklist for external marketers of training products and services (table 1-4).

Table 1-2. A survey for training marketers internal to organizations.

Circle the number that best represents to what extent the following statements are true:
1 = to no extent; 2 = to a slight extent; 3 = to a moderate extent; 4 = to a great extent.

1.	Senior management embraces development publicly.	1	2	3	4
2.	The training function knows on what criteria it will determine its priorities.	1	2	3	4
3.	The training budget is more than 2 percent of payroll, or the total annual training expenditure per employee exceeds $600.	1	2	3	4
4.	There is decentralized authority.	1	2	3	4
5.	Training is tied into other organizational/HR systems.	1	2	3	4

(continued on next page)

Table 1-2. A survey for training marketers internal to organizations (continued).

6.	Your training operation includes individuals with creative talents and good communication skills.	1	2	3	4
7.	Your culture tolerates mistakes and promotes learning from failures.	1	2	3	4
8.	You have a coordinated training department plan.	1	2	3	4
9.	You have technology in place to track the effectiveness and completion rates of training, as well as to handle registration and logistics.	1	2	3	4
10.	More than 40 percent of employees participate in development offerings.	1	2	3	4
11.	Your training function has its own mission, strategy, and priorities.	1	2	3	4
12.	You are given time to devote to marketing.	1	2	3	4
13.	Creative thinking and innovation are promoted organizationally.	1	2	3	4
14.	There is a uniform look and feel for materials from your department.	1	2	3	4
15.	You have a pool of tried-and-true facilitators and suppliers you can rely on.	1	2	3	4
16.	All levels of management facilitate learning and promote development activities.	1	2	3	4
17.	You have communicated the vision of a learning organization and plans to move in that direction.	1	2	3	4
18.	You have state-of-the-art tools to do your marketing, ranging from a graphic design program to a fast computer.	1	2	3	4
19.	You know where the organization is headed.	1	2	3	4
20.	You measure learning and demonstrate learning successes.	1	2	3	4
21.	You remain connected with the outside world in your industry and the field of training and development.	1	2	3	4
22.	You are seen by the organization as a clearinghouse of ideas and resources.	1	2	3	4
23.	Many ways of sharing knowledge are utilized (e.g., job rotation, on-the-job training, and cross-functional teams).	1	2	3	4
24.	You have free or inexpensive facilities in which to present new ideas to different segments of the employee population.	1	2	3	4
25.	Your organization continuously adapts, improves, and learns.	1	2	3	4
26.	The training function involves employee input at all levels.	1	2	3	4
27.	You have in-house printing capabilities or a working relationship with a printer.	1	2	3	4
28.	There is accountability for ongoing development on an employee or managerial level.	1	2	3	4
29.	You have well-defined and developed products and services.	1	2	3	4
30.	You use electronic job aids and just-in-time learning technologies.	1	2	3	4

Organizational Readiness Audit for Internals

Now, transfer the numbers you have circled for each item on the audit to the scoring grid in table 1-3. Add the scores in each column and enter them in the total row at the bottom of the grid. The highest possible score for each column is 40.

A high score in the second column indicates that your organization is one that possesses qualities of a learning organization. Development is embraced, mistakes are tolerated, learning occurs at all levels. In these organizations, marketing is relatively simple as employees are already committed to ongoing learning.

A high score in the fourth column indicates that your training function is aligned with other organizational systems and processes. People attend training because it is part of their individual development plan or because it is a requirement to move to the next organizational level. Training is institutionalized, and marketing is received by a motivated audience.

A high score in the sixth column indicates that you have the necessary resources for marketing: individuals with the necessary competencies and skill sets, funding, and technology. In combination with high scores in either of the previous areas, a high score here bodes well for the success of your marketing efforts.

Table 1-3. Scoring grid for the organizational readiness audit.

Category: Learning Organization		Category: Aligned Training Function		Category: Marketing Resources	
Question #	Your Rating	Question #	Your Rating	Question #	Your Rating
1		2		3	
4		5		6	
7		8		9	
10		11		12	
13		14		15	
16		17		18	
19		20		21	
22		23		24	
25		26		27	
28		29		30	
Total		Total		Total	

Chapter 3 focuses on the transformation that many organizations still need to undergo in order to receive high scores in all three of these areas.

Organizational Checklist for Externals

Table 1-4 can help you, as an external trainer, determine if you have the business skills, networking connections, resources, and materials to meet the needs of your client organizations.

Table 1-4. A marketing readiness checklist for external trainers.

The Business Side of Your Business

Check the box to the left if you have:

☐ A written business plan

☐ A defined target audience, industry, or company profile?

☐ Monthly contact with clients or potential clients

☐ A measurement system in place

☐ Knowledge of local industry

☐ Well-defined and developed products and services

☐ A captivating company name, logo, or both

☐ A tagline that captures the essence of the work you do in a sentence (or less)

☐ A unique selling proposition, something that sets your business apart from the rest

☐ A brand identity, an element that links your materials so that recipients easily recognize that they are yours

☐ Knowledge of training and development so that you can "talk the talk" with clients or potential clients

☐ Knowledge of the industry you work in

Networking

Check the box to the left if you have:

☐ A name for yourself so that people seek you out

☐ A list of companies in your target area—industry or geography

☐ A Rolodex of key players in local organizations

☐ Partnerships with reliable suppliers in related or competing organizations to which you can refer clients

☐ A list of local associations/local association memberships

☐ Membership in key industry groups

☐ People to partner with who possess skills in the competency areas in which you are lacking, whether at your company or external to your company

---

Resources

Check the box to the left if you have:

- ☐ A professional office setup (e.g., no busy signal when clients call, a fax, separate email accounts for your personal and business purposes, and possibly a Website)
- ☐ A budget for marketing
- ☐ Close to a quarter of your time (or staff time) set aside to devote to marketing
- ☐ A database for tracking clients

Materials

Check the box to the left if you have:

- ☐ Templates for a project plan, proposals, invoices, and other forms
- ☐ Testimonials and references on file
- ☐ A portfolio and samples
- ☐ Free or inexpensive facilities you can use for meetings, workshops, and other business purposes
- ☐ Lists of clients, projects, speaking engagements, and publications
- ☐ A professional bio prepared in three formats (one to two sentences, single paragraph, single page) and readily available for sending at a moment's notice
- ☐ A digital and hard copy black-and-white or color photograph of yourself
- ☐ Letterhead, business cards
- ☐ A price list (in your mind or on paper)
- ☐ Graphic design software application
- ☐ A portable demonstration or preview of your products and services

---

Add the number of items you've checked in each section, and enter that number in the second row in table 1-5.

If your score is low in the first area, you might want to slow down your development and marketing of new programs until you can devote some time to the big-picture issues that affect your business. Where do you want your company to go? What are your goals? What unique offering do you want to provide and to whom do you wish to provide it? Several good books on running your own business are included in the References and Additional Resources sections.

If your score is low in the second column, you need to develop and enhance some key relationships. Relationship building for externals is the focus of chapter 4. You might also wish to read further on the topic of networking—an often overlooked and misunderstood art.

If your lowest score is in either the area of resources or materials, you might need to take some time to focus on the logistical and administrative aspects of your

Table 1-5. Analyze your marketing readiness checklist.

Business Side of Your Business	
Fill in the number of items you checked for this area in the blank to the right	___ out of 12 possible
Is the gap between your score and the highest score: *** = huge * = moderate 0 = nonexistent	

Networking	
Fill in the number of items you checked for this area in the blank to the right	___ out of 7 possible
Is the gap between your score and the highest score: *** = huge * = moderate 0 = nonexistent	

Resources	
Fill in the number of items you checked for this area in the blank to the right	___ out of 4 possible
Is the gap between your score and the highest score: *** = huge * = moderate 0 = nonexistent	

Materials	
Fill in the number of items you checked for this area in the blank to the right	___ out of 11 possible
Is the gap between your score and the highest score: *** = huge * = moderate 0 = nonexistent	

business. Developing these resources is a long-term investment that really pays off when your marketing efforts enable you to respond quickly to a great demand for your products and services.

* * *

Clearly, whether you're internal or external, you can accomplish your marketing without all of these factors in place, but marketing in an organization where most of these factors exist will be much easier. And, theoretically, working on these things isn't just an exercise for marketing. It will help your business or the reputation of your department as a whole.

You'll have a chance to work on many of these factors in this book, but if you need additional help getting your business infrastructure or training function in place, several good books about consulting or managing a training function are listed in the Resources section.

Regardless of your starting point, you've picked this book up, so you must already recognize the importance of your marketing role or are already looking at ways to get better at it. Good luck in this worthy endeavor!

What Is My Role in Marketing?

I think I realized that I had to be a marketer when I was five years old and began selling lemonade as my first business. My approach today is much different than most people, who will tell you that they love to do "the thing" they do, but they don't like having to sell it. I have always seen it as a happy obligation to let people know what I have to offer. After all, if you have taken the time to be excellent at something, don't you owe it to others who are looking for excellence to let them know? Think about how much time and energy you have been saved by someone being aware of exactly the thing you were looking for and being able to direct you there. Rather than an imposition, it is a terrific gift to you. When I was five and selling my lemonade, what I needed to know was this: "If I know the people that are thirsty right now and can tell them about my stand, both of us will be happy." Translate that to your work.

Nance Cheifetz, corporate fairy godmother, A Sense of Delight

---

 ### Now What?

With what ideas or actionable ideas should you walk away from this chapter?

- You can't ignore your role as a marketer.
    - If you're a trainer internal to an organization your marketing role is to promote the value of specific training initiatives, the training function, and the concept of training as a whole.

— If you're an external supplier or consultant, your marketing role is to promote yourself through strong client relationships and to show how your products and services fill an organizational need.

- The benefits of marketing include increased credibility and visibility and fewer battles for clients, resources, and participation.

- Look for opportunities to strengthen your marketing competencies:
  — relationship building
  — comprehension of organizational and individual behavior
  — knowledge of your audience
  — knowledge of your specific topic/field
  — creativity
  — intellectual versatility
  — cost-benefit analysis
  — analysis
  — questioning technique
  — project planning
  — maintenance/evaluation
  — written and verbal presentation
  — graphic design
  — computer proficiency.

- *Internals:* Be aware of any opportunities for you to promote a learning organization, to align the training function with organizational business strategies, or to beef up the organization's marketing resources.

- *Externals:* Make sure that in addition to developing high-quality products and services, you devote enough time and resources to managing the business side of your business, increasing your visibility in your field and in the community, and developing marketing tools.

Chapter Two

Addressing Motivation: **Your Learners'**

* *

 ## A **Quick** Look

When learners show little interest in one of our products or services, we throw up our hands and exclaim, "They asked for it!" or "Their managers say they need it." "Why," we ask, "aren't they taking advantage of it?" But, the real question isn't why they aren't doing what they said they would, but why they would consider it in the first place. When we market from the positive perspective of what motivates people, we are more likely to get appropriate, interested, and dedicated participants for our interventions. Motivational factors include the desire for personal or professional growth, the fact that development is valued organizationally, and a strong correlation between training and career opportunities. Analytical tools help us find the unique motivators of our target audience.

Chapter **Features**

* Eleven learner motivators and five de-motivators

* Sample questions and tools for determining learner motivation

* Marketing competencies addressed:
— Relationship-building
— Comprehension of organizational and individual behavior
— Analysis
— Questioning technique

Eleven Learner Motivators

The movie *Field of Dreams* made "If you build it, they will come" a household expression. It worked for Kevin Costner's character and his ball field, but when it comes to your training and development initiatives, don't count on it. No matter how well designed or customized your product or service is, its mere existence will not draw people to it. So what motivates individuals to utilize your products and services? What motivates people to invest in their development? Here's a list of 11 key motivators that should help you answer these questions:

1. *There's a clear connection between training and the work they do:* When employees see an immediate value in participating, resistance to participation drops away.
2. *They value personal growth:* Some people are avid learners who constantly take advantage of opportunities to grow and learn new things.
3. *It's required:* Whether to meet industry standards, to absolve the company from legal responsibility, or to perform one's job, learners are expected to participate in certain mandatory programs.
4. *It's tied to career advancement:* Career growth opportunities for those completing an intervention, or a series of interventions, provide tangible benefits of program completion.
5. *Training is valued organizationally:* Once an organization becomes a learning organization, the question is no longer how can one make time to invest in development, but how can one not make that investment?
6. *Learners receive recognition for completion:* People like to be recognized, whether that recognition is formal or informal, major or minor.
7. *Classroom interventions are opportunities to meet others:* Many employees appreciate the opportunity for individuals across departments and across levels to interact on equal footing. If the classroom is a public one, they

might also appreciate meeting others with similar responsibilities outside their organizations.

8. *Stepping away from work often invigorates people:* Some people just relish the opportunity for a change of pace and return to work recharged and rededicated.

9. *They've had positive experiences with training in the past:* When people's investment in training has really paid off, they are more likely to try it again.

10. *They are compensated for participation:* Financial rewards for completing an intervention or series of interventions are short-term motivators that can be effective in certain circumstances.

11. *The training was marketed well:* Good marketing is, in and of itself, a draw.

A Closer Look at Learner Motivators

Now, consider some specific ways you can use these 11 motivators to your advantage when designing and marketing your training interventions.

1. THERE'S A CLEAR CONNECTION BETWEEN TRAINING AND THE WORK THEY DO. Employees will take advantage of opportunities to learn skills that they need to do their jobs more efficiently. Participants' supervisors will also more readily support their participation in programs that make them immediately more productive. In a recent study conducted by ASTD and the MASIE Center (2001) on the success of e-learning initiatives, the single largest motivator for voluntary learners was the desire to obtain new skills for current or future job opportunities.

To provide training that is linked directly to what employees do or will be doing, you need to be aware of the competencies required for various positions and on strategic initiatives planned for your organization. This also means that scenarios and examples used in marketing materials have to be true to the employee's experience and position.

This motivator is so strong that it can override some common de-motivators. During a recent needs assessment, employees of a nonprofit organization were asked what prevented them from investing in their development. The primary response was lack of time. "You mean to tell me," they were countered, "that you could not make time if the development opportunity in front of you was immediately relevant and valuable?" It turns out what prevented them from attending wasn't time at all but that training didn't add value for them.

In times when change is obvious—an individual has been given a new job, new responsibilities, or a new reporting structure—it is easier for employees to connect training with enhanced job performance. At other times, marketing will need to help employees become aware of that connection. Marketing might need to make learners aware of their "blind spots"—areas in which they need to improve but don't already know it. For example, "Are you one of those Excel users who counts the number of items in a column because you don't know how to make the program count them for you?" or, "Last week, only one out of 10 secret shoppers in our retail outlets was properly instructed on using our 'Do It Yourself' kiosk. Do you know how to address customer questions at the kiosk?"

What Motivates Me to Invest in My Development?

If I see training as just a "feel good" session, then I won't bother with it. If it's simple skill build-ing, I'm more likely to participate. It depends if I think I need the new skills.

Eric Aboaf, partner, Bain & Company

---

2. **THEY VALUE PERSONAL GROWTH.** Some people are ready for any opportunity to acquire new knowledge or skills. They will be at your programs regardless of the topic, even if they don't really need to know it.

You want to be careful not to gear all your marketing (or, for that matter, all your offerings) to this self-selected group. If you get all your data on what programs employees would like to see from those who attend your current programs, you are skewing your data. You'll also have problems when your marketing efforts are so successful that your programs are standing room only. You'll need to consider whether this group of eager participants should be limited to a certain number of courses they can attend per calendar year, or whether only those with real business needs for a particular topic can attend a workshop on that topic. Alternatively, you may wish to determine registration priority according to some criterion other than first-come, first-served.

What Motivates Me to Invest in My Development?

I guess you could say I'm a lifelong learner. I am constantly trying to learn those things that "I don't know that I don't know." I try to make time for development. I consider it maintenance for my mind.

Shari Albert, executive coach, Inspiring Minds Coaching

---

3. **IT'S REQUIRED.** Employees usually complete training that is required, sometimes grudgingly, but usually without fail. The marketing of mandatory programs, then, has a different focus than for most voluntary programs: to increase learner satis-faction, not to increase start rates. For example, "Annual training on preventing

sexual harassment is necessary not only to protect our company from costly lawsuits, but because we don't want any of our employees to have to work in a hostile environment. We are committed to your security." It must highlight the "What's in it for me" to participate: "Current licensing on Microsoft Office programs will make you extremely employable, as well as allowing you to work more efficiently on our new systems."

Marketing must also help supervisors understand why the training is required so that they will not be reluctant to release the employee to participate. In addition, marketing can help supervisors feel that their needs have also been taken into account. For example, "We know it will be hard for you to send your entire staff to mandatory safety training. That's why we're holding multiple sessions at various times during the day. ABC Company is committed to helping you get all employees through this training because we'll all benefit when we reduce workplace accidents."

What Motivates Me to Invest in My Development?

I am in a profession where technology advances very quickly. Such issues as energy conservation were hardly discussed when I received my architectural training 40 years ago. My professional licensing organization also believes ongoing development is important and has set up mandatory requirements to keep one's architectural license current. This obligation has provided more training opportunities, although many of the new courses are geared to those who are attending for the "learning units," not the learning.

Theodore Liebman, FAIA, Liebman Melting Partnership Architects and Planners

---

4. TRAINING IS TIED TO CAREER ADVANCEMENT. Companies that are recognized as the leaders in developing their people have clearly established career management systems in place. Professional growth and new challenges become the norm in these organizations. Lateral moves are encouraged as much as vertical moves, as they are opportunities to learn and use new skills. Training can support people who make these moves and who are actively invested in their careers. Marketing for this type of training should highlight the ways it can prepare people for career changes and spell out the competencies that will be acquired in the program.

5. TRAINING IS VALUED ORGANIZATIONALLY. In organizations that place a high value on training and that create a strong sense of personal responsibility for one's own development, the question isn't how to get people to invest in training, it's how to keep up with demand. Creating this type of organization is the focus of chapter 3.

Myth: Trained people will leave.

Fact: People don't generally leave organizations because they know too much or because they are too well trained. They leave when what they know is not put to use or valued by the organization. Some people are put off by marketing that stresses the acquisition of skills that will keep people employable. To them, that sort of campaign gives trained employees permission to leave the organization that trained them. This is a management or a career development issue, but it is not a reason to not provide training. Trained employees will leave, as will untrained employees, and when they do, they take their appreciation of the organization that trained them. It is hoped that the organization will replace them with someone who was trained elsewhere so that investments in development will come back around.

---

6. **LEARNERS RECEIVE RECOGNITION FOR COMPLETION.** Robert Mager has conducted extensive research on human needs. One need that continually rises toward the top is the need for appreciation. Recognizing an individual for his or her investment in ongoing development is a great motivator. Recognition can be big or small, formal or informal. Eligibility for a promotion after completing all of your new hire certification requirements is big and formal; a framed certificate of completion is small; a word of congratulations at a staff meeting is informal. Your marketing materials, both leading up to and following a training intervention, should include language that recognizes the individual's investment. For example, a sentence on your course confirmation communication might read, "Congratulations! Signing up for Spanish language instruction indicates that you are committed to working more effectively with our growing Latino customer base!"

7. **CLASSROOM INTERVENTIONS ARE OPPORTUNITIES TO MEET OTHERS.** When training is offered across internal departments, people often relish the opportunity to meet others, to get a better feel for the organization as a whole, and to put faces with voices and names. Recent studies have found that community building within organizations is very important to employee motivation and productivity as people who are engaged in their work environment feel a heightened sense of responsibility and work harder.

Be sure to mention class size in your marketing when it is either intimate (and people will really get a chance to bond with other participants) or huge (and people will have multiple networking opportunities). When classroom training is offered in a public forum, emphasize that participants will meet others who do similar work for other organizations and have an opportunity to learn from their successes and experiences.

8. **STEPPING AWAY FROM WORK OFTEN INVIGORATES PEOPLE.** Some people just enjoy the fact that training is a break in their routines. They don't care too much about the topic; motivational speakers or topics of general interest appeal to this group. An energetic and fun program is just what some people need to get back to work refreshed and productive. During especially turbulent times, bringing in some inspiring speakers and facilitators to discuss what's going on can be a huge morale boost.

9. **THEY'VE HAD POSITIVE EXPERIENCES WITH TRAINING IN THE PAST.** The best predictor of future performance is past performance. The same holds true for predicting the likelihood that a training opportunity will be positive. In the ASTD and MASIE Center e-learning study, 72 percent reported an overall positive experience and, of these, 84 percent said they were willing to take a similar online course in the future.

An advantage of a past positive experience with training for your marketing efforts is that those individuals who've had a good experience with training become ambassadors for your subsequent programs. On the flipside, a bad experience in training can be a long-lasting de-motivator.

10. **THEY ARE COMPENSATED FOR PARTICIPATION.** Some companies tie merit or pay increases directly to the number of hours of training an employee completes. Sometimes, employees cannot move to better-compensated positions without completing a course of study. The problem with taking employees' desire for compensation as the motivator for your programs is that individuals don't necessarily feel a need for training, just for the rewards that training brings. Additionally, company-offered training should be viewed as a benefit in and of itself and to pay people to attend free training on company time is to discount it.

11. **THE TRAINING WAS MARKETED WELL.** Marketing itself is a draw, when done well. Intense marketing and promotion was a key factor in successfully achieving full participation in several of the courses in the ASTD/MASIE Center e-learning study. Yet marketing for its own sake will only work once. Your programs have to live up to the promises made in your marketing campaign, or your audience won't trust you in the future. So, don't use marketing to draw people to programs that aren't geared for them or that are not well designed.

Five Learner De-Motivators

So, what prevents people from participating in developmental opportunities? Many de-motivators simply are the converse of motivators, for example:

Myth: People come for the free food.

Fact: Food (coffee and donuts), prizes, or gifts are nice perks that might appeal to learners, but they are not motivators that would help someone decide to embark on a program. In fact, individuals who participate in programs that embrace the other motivators discussed in this chapter—such as programs that are immediately valuable to them—don't really care if they have to go out and buy food or whether it's brought in.

This isn't to say you shouldn't provide food or send participants trinkets as part of your marketing campaign. Giveaways can add fun and intrigue to a marketing campaign, like the plastic wedding rings given out by two merging consulting companies prior to their first shared meeting or the Legos building blocks sent out with invitations to a "Building a Better Organization Through Better Relationships" conference.

Participants aren't compensated or rewarded; employee development is not valued in the organization as a whole; learners don't see a direct link to the work that they do; or they have had bad experiences in the past. You must be aware, though, of other key de-motivators that can undermine your training efforts, namely:

1. *There is no accountability:* It is extremely de-motivating when there isn't any tracking of who has completed what, or when no "credit" is granted.
2. *Learners are uncomfortable with the learning methodology:* Even when participants say that they want learning to come to them on their own time, many are still uncomfortable with the technologies that can make that possible.
3. *Learners cannot get off work for training:* Very real, logistical concerns, including lack of time and coverage, can stand in the way of people's desire to invest in their development.
4. *The time or location is bad:* Getting everyone together in one place at one time can be a real challenge for classroom training.
5. *They don't lack motivation, they just don't need training:* Training is not the answer for everyone.

A Closer Look at Learner De-Motivators

It's important as you design and market your training interventions that you are aware of five important factors that de-motivate learners.

1. THERE IS NO ACCOUNTABILITY. When courses are required, it is de-motivating if penalties aren't assessed for participants who do not attend, or if those who do aren't rewarded. Similarly, if no one holds participants accountable for their new learning, or if there are no opportunities to use newly acquired skills, people feel as if their time and efforts were wasted. Even if they had a positive impression of the program on completion, it will sour when workplace reality doesn't support the learning. Marketing must include educating the supervisors of participants on how to utilize the employees' new knowledge back on the job. Marketing also includes sharing the results of the session (evaluation reports, test scores, and so forth) with supervisors and senior management after the fact.

2.   LEARNERS ARE UNCOMFORTABLE WITH THE LEARNING METHODOLOGY. As much as training professionals want to utilize training solutions that are just-in-time and cutting-edge, they can't leave their learners behind. The solution in many companies is to offer blended training by which parts are delivered in conventional, tried formats and other parts are delivered via technology. Marketing must stress that learners have support and aren't on their own when they are completing training in the absence of an instructor.

3.   LEARNERS CANNOT GET OFF WORK FOR TRAINING. Sometimes managers won't, or can't, allow employees time to train. Or, employees may feel too responsible to take the time when they know what stress it will put their colleagues under. Training professionals can help create coverage plans, help pay for related overtime expenses, and provide several offerings in a day of classroom training. Trainers should survey employees about when they want to complete training. If employees indicate a willingness to invest their own time, trainers should make sure some programs are offered on employees' own time.

Sometimes, even when employees make the time for training, they cannot get off work. J.J. Cutler, a senior executive at an international manufacturing company, says it is a big disincentive when "work continues to pile up while I'm in training. Sometimes I attend courses and spend the whole time in the hall on my cell phone. Then I go home and spend the whole evening catching up on my email." Even when participants are given training to complete at their desks it is stressful when customers and co-workers, who don't realize that they are training, continue to interrupt them.

4.   THE TIME OR LOCATION IS BAD. You will never be able to please everyone when it comes to scheduling classroom training, but offering it at various times and in various locations will help motivate those individuals who continuously are unable to participate due to scheduling conflicts. Experiment with alternative scheduling—

like offering full-day programs across two half-days. And, bring training to employees on the job whenever feasible. For a large pharmaceutical company's sales reps, for example, training was provided via audiotape that they could listen to in their cars between sales calls.

5. THEY DON'T LACK MOTIVATION, THEY JUST DON'T NEED TRAINING. Training professionals also have to be willing to accept that there are people for whom no motivation is going to work. For those who may be close to retiring, who have just completed an extensive degree program, who have many personal issues, the choice not to train may be the most appropriate one.

Identifying Motivators and De-Motivators

Being aware of learner motivators and de-motivators is an important starting point, but it would be wrong to assume that you understand what motivates members of your target audience without asking them. Because motivators shift or are situational, making assumptions about your audience's level of motivation or of what will motivate them can backfire. For example, you might assume that individuals don't want to participate and overplay that "fact," leading those who participate of their own free will feeling defensive and those who have been forced to be there feeling berated.

So, talk to people regularly about how motivated they are and about what motivates them. As a training professional, you are already used to talking to people continuously about their needs. You probably also often remember to ask them about their expectations for your training products and services.

With questions like the ones in figure 2-1, you can expand your questioning repertoire to include questions that get at people's motivation and at their view of training and development as a whole and not just in regard to a specific initiative or business need. When you can get this type of information, it is extra ammunition you can use in your marketing. And, answers to these questions can help you with a lot more than just marketing. This information can help you prepare facilitators, design programs, reset expectations, create rewards for completion, get buy-in for integrating training into larger organizational systems, and adjust program logistics.

You can find many opportunities to ask questions like the ones posed in figure 2-1, including the following:

- *during needs assessments you are already conducting:* Just be sure that your assessments involve employees at all different stages and levels in their careers, not just self-selected, or highly motivated employees.

**Figure 2-1. Sample questions for eliciting information
about motivators and de-motivators.**

Which of the following was a motivator for you to participate in this program?

☐ It was required
☐ It might lead to career advancement
☐ Thought I would learn something about a topic that would help me at work
☐ Heard speaker before
☐ It was recommended to me by my manager/colleague/other (circle one)
☐ Other (describe): _____

Which of these would motivate you to develop yourself? (Select as many as apply.)

☐ Increased compensation
☐ Tie to career advancement
☐ Recognition from management for completing courses
☐ Recognition from colleagues/customers for completing courses
☐ Free lunch
☐ Other (describe): _____

What would motivate you to invest in your development, in an ideal world?

What motivates you to invest in your development, considering your time, budget, and other restraints?

How motivated are you to attend this program?

☐ Highly
☐ Well
☐ Slightly
☐ Not at all

How motivated are you to invest in your professional development?

☐ Highly, I am a lifelong learner
☐ Well, I think ongoing learning is a important tool for acquiring new skills
☐ Slightly, there are some topics that training can teach
☐ Not at all, I'm where I want to be professionally or I can learn what I need to know on the job

NOTE: This is a good question to use as a sort when you are conducting any kind of assessment. For example, instead of just reporting that 100 employees want training on leadership skills, you can report data this way: 100 employees want training on leadership; of these, 98 are individuals who are, in general, highly motivated to invest in their development. Or, you could say that 100 employees want training on leadership, regardless of their level of motivation to develop themselves in general.

Is the training and development provided by ABC Organization motivating?

Do you consider opportunities for development a perk of working here?

Would you weigh the opportunities for development here in your decision about whether to remain working here?

I would be motivated to invest in my development: (Check all that apply.)

- ☐ Only if free and on company time
- ☐ If free even if it's on my own time
- ☐ On my own time if it's paid for by the organization
- ☐ On a topic of personal interest
- ☐ Only on topics that are immediately relevant to my job
- ☐ On any business topic, even if not immediately relevant to my job

---

You are a member of the target audience for the customer service intervention. Why didn't you choose to take advantage of it?

What prevents you from taking classes? (Select as many as apply.)

- ☐ No time
- ☐ No coverage for me
- ☐ Inconvenient location
- ☐ My supervisor doesn't support requests for development
- ☐ Can't locate appropriate classes
- ☐ Training is not tied to my career development
- ☐ Development not valued
- ☐ Other (describe): _____

You signed up for this workshop after receiving an email invitation. Which of these motivators were highlighted in the email you received? (Check as many as apply.)

- ☐ Increased compensation
- ☐ Tie to career advancement
- ☐ Recognition from management on completion of courses
- ☐ Recognition from colleagues/customers on completion of courses
- ☐ Other (describe): _____

Did the mention of these motivators in the marketing appeal to you?

(continued on next page)

**Figure 2-1. Sample questions for eliciting information
about motivators and de-motivators (continued).**

Which of these things motivate you in general? (Check as many as apply.)

☐ Learning
☐ Interacting with others
☐ Creating something new
☐ Having fun
☐ Doing a good job
☐ Spending time with my family
☐ Getting recognition
☐ Making money
☐ Other (describe): _____

Which of these would you like to receive as a reward for completing a program like this one? (Check as many as apply.)

☐ A certificate of completion
☐ A gift certificate (Where? _____)
☐ A book by the facilitator
☐ A day off
☐ A round of applause from my boss
☐ Other (describe: _____)
☐ I don't need any rewards

- *at organization-wide gatherings:* When you are out promoting your department, or your upcoming programs and offerings, collect some data, too. Distribute postcard-sized surveys and put all completed surveys in a raffle drawing.
- *at staff meetings:* Bring your message out to the participants as often as possible and with it, your questions. This is important at big departments and active departments, as well as departments that traditionally do not avail themselves of much in the way of organizational training.
- *on registration forms:* If learners have to fill in fields on the computer or on paper to sign up for a class, take the opportunity to add an extra question about motivation or about their overall perception of training.
- *on course confirmations:* Use the confirmation to highlight motivators and to get feedback on what motivated them to sign up for the program you are confirming.
- *with a telephone call to those who register or to the managers of those who are registered:* Making contact by voice is a great way to elicit motivators and de-motivators, as well as an opportunity to ask follow-up questions to learn more specific information.

- *at the start of a program:* You want to ask what motivated participants to attend a program at its start because if you ask them at the end, their answer may well have changed as a result of what was covered during the program. Also, you tend to have more time at the start (even before the program begins officially) than you have at the end when everyone is in a rush to leave. It's also a good warm-up exercise that gets people comfortable being involved in the training.
- *through follow-up with those who should have participated (members of your target audience) but did not:* Call or email these individuals to learn what de-motivators may be at work.

You'll learn a lot by asking potential learners what motivates them to invest in their development. But, you may have to ask more than once before you get at the real motivator at hand.

Finally, another effective way to learn about motivators for developmental opportunities is to ask yourself. Just slow down sometime, and ask yourself what would motivate *you* to invest in *your own* development. Chances are your response will be the same as that of plenty of members of your target audience.

What Motivates Me to Invest in My Development?

It's simple: I am my own best investment. I could state the obvious: to network, to stay at the forefront of innovation in my field of study, or because it's fun. Those statements are all true. If, however, I do not invest in myself, how can I develop into tomorrow's innovative thinker? I've always enjoyed discovery, the learning process, and the wealth of experience that's out there. What motivates me to attend training programs is the belief that this program might bring me closer to a new insight, a new discovery, or an idea that in and of itself really excites me.

Lorena Melghem, executive assistant, Greylock Partners

 ### Now What?

With what ideas or actionable ideas should you walk away from this chapter?

- Marketing needs to appeal to what would motivate someone to invest his or her time in your training opportunities.
- Don't make assumptions about the level or focus of your target audience's motivation. Use questions that uncover what motivates or de-motivates your learners at every opportunity.

- Respond to the following questions to capitalize on the motivators discussed in this chapter:

  — Is there a clear connection between what will be covered in the program to the work that actual audience members do?

  — What kind of personal growth might an individual who completes your program experience?

  — Should your program be mandatory or elective? If mandatory, how will you make it palatable to and create positive expectations for your participants?

  — Are there any career advancement benefits to completing your program?

  — What mechanisms are in place for participants to receive formal or informal recognition upon completion?

  — Are opportunities to interact with others included in the program?

  — Is the program invigorating so that participants return to work recharged?

  — If your learners have had negative experiences with training in the past, have you given them an opportunity to vent those concerns, and have you assured them that they have been addressed?

  — Did you remember to market your program?

  — Are you able to assist the department whose employees will be attending your program with coverage in any way?

  — Have you scheduled programs in multiple locations and during various time periods?

  — Have you addressed the comfort level of participants and put into place any opportunities to increase their comfort level prior to participation?

  — Have you helped the participant (and the participant's supervisor) understand his or her responsibilities in completing your program?

  — Have you identified any audiences for whom this course would not add value for whatever reason and excused them, in your mind, from participating?

  — Are you working to establish training as a value-added function organizationally? Doing so is the focus of chapter 3.

Chapter Three

Addressing Motivation:
Your Organization's

✳✳

A **Quick Look**

An organization's commitment to training and development can be placed on a spectrum. At one end of this spectrum, training isn't valued organizationally; often it is the first item cut from an organization's budget when times are tough. At the other end of the spectrum, training's positive contribution to the bottom line is distinctly understood, and the chief executive officer (CEO) holds individuals at all levels accountable for participation in developmental activities. Clearly, marketing in organizations near this latter end of the spectrum is easier than it is in organizations near the other end. The focus of this chapter is on how to move your organization toward the end of the spectrum that supports development as a concept and in which marketing activities are relatively easy to incorporate.

Chapter **Features**

* Tips for ensuring that training is a value-added function in your organization
* Examples of companies that are committed to development as a concept
* Marketing competencies addressed:
  — Relationship building
  — Comprehension of organizational and individual behavior
  — Analysis
  — Questioning techniques

Become a Learning Organization

Marketing training and development initiatives to an organization that values employee development is far easier and more enjoyable than in an organization where employee development isn't given importance. In organizations where a commitment to learning exists, trainers rarely have to fight for money, time, or other resources. These organizations have seen and profited from the positive benefits of training in solving their core business problems and now see training as a solution. *In short, creating a workplace that understands the value of employee development is the best possible marketing tool.*

How do you promote development as a concept in organizations? How do you create an organization committed to ongoing development and learning? Table 3-1 shows you what you must do.

How does an organization make this shift? Read on as each item in the right-hand column of table 3-1 is described in more detail.

Training Is Integrated

Training is most effective when it occurs as part of an interconnected system of workplace policies and practices designed to improve performance. If training activities are going on independently of other organizational systems, individuals within that organization tend to question whether training really matters. For example, an obvious sign of a disconnect between training and other organizational systems is present when performance review data is not utilized to determine specific training needs or to make employees accountable for developing in the areas identified as their opportunities for improvement. Clearly, the performance data points to organizational or individual needs, and if training offerings don't address these needs, one or both of the processes will be perceived as weak with little accountability.

Table 3-1. Becoming a learning organization.

You need to make the shift . . .	
from here . . .	**. . . to here**
Training is a stand-alone endeavor. Learning is not tied to other organizational systems such as performance management or career development.	Training is integrated; it is part of all organizational systems and strategic initiatives.
Training is content-driven. For example, "Wouldn't a workshop on diversity be neat?"	Training and development initiatives are driven by business strategy. For example, "Customer satisfaction surveys indicate that we don't understand their culture; diversity training will help us connect with our customers' experiences."
Evaluation is based on ratings. For example, smile sheets are used to determine what participants thought of our programs.	Evaluation is tied to business and performance measures for a more objective and quantitative rating.
Decision making is centralized. Decisions about employee development needs and priorities are made within the training function—without much input from the managers and employees.	Decision making is customer-driven. Decisions about employee development needs and priorities are made by members of the target audience and their supervisors.
The training function is accountable for organizational learning and development.	Individuals at all levels in the organization are accountable for development.
Training occurs in a classroom.	Training occurs anywhere and everywhere via a menu of alternative delivery methods.
Training is funded annually.	Training utilizes a fee-for-service model in which training is purchased by the users who recognize its value and are happy to pay for it.

On the flipside, when training offerings and budgets are constructed directly from performance data for current and future needs, there is tremendous accountability as trainers become responsible for plugging gaps and as organizations realize that cutting training budgets has a direct impact on existing organizational performance gaps.

Other workplace policies and practices that can and should be linked to the practices of your training function include the use of self-directed work teams and cross-training; and compensation practices, such as profit sharing, stock ownership, and team-based or incentive compensation. When these programs are in place within an organization, yet training isn't linked to them, it appears that the training element is ineffectual. For example, when self-directed work teams and team-based incentives are in place, training on individual-based skills would not be appropriate; training on process improvement for workgroups might be.

Training should be so aligned with an organization's systems and culture that training becomes a source of "brand-building" for the company. Appropriate learning strategies and formats integrate the brand experience that the organization promises its customers. Hardly coincidentally, this concept was first promoted by the Disney Corporation where all employees are immersed in the Disney brand experience as part of their ongoing development. Employees can't deliver an experience they haven't had. Disney views its trainers as bearers of the organization's culture, who are intimately familiar with the brand promise of the organization, and who, through training, are able to bring it to life.

Driven by Business Strategy

Training should not only be linked to existing programs and systems. Training must be driven by business needs—current and future.

According to Dean Spitzer and Malcolm Conway (2002) of IBM Learning Services, "Training is in the midst of a crisis that some contend threatens its very survival. Simply stated, the crisis is the failure to show that investing in training produces demonstrable business results." Trainers continually should ask questions to understand an organization's priorities and strategies: Where is the organization headed? Who is ready to go there? Who needs support or enhanced skills to get there? How is institutional knowledge preserved and transferred? How are diamonds in the rough identified?

Make organizational priorities the focus of your training function. You might also use your knowledge to influence what organization priorities should be. Use your knowledge of workplace, workforce, and population trends to demonstrate

---

How Conoco Links Training to Business Strategy

Under the umbrella of Conoco University, a wide range of programs has been designed to create and sustain a continuous learning environment with Conoco. This benefits the company and responds to skill gaps identified by the staffing and development process. Conoco University addresses a variety of critical development challenges, ranging from enhancing business literacy skills to first line supervisor training to developing visionary leaders at the executive level.

Conoco's performance management process integrates business plans with the pursuit of individual goals. Inherent in the process is accountability for not only achieving results, but also doing so in a way that supports our core values and enables employees to develop new skills. Underpinning the process is a variety of reinforcement tools that support achievement and development.

Conoco's 1998 annual report

the connection between business strategy and employee development. For example, U.S. census data predicts that the Latino population will be the largest segment of the population in 2010. Is your organization capturing its share of this large and growing market? Does your research and development department understand the needs of the Latino population? How could your employees more effectively sell to Latinos? Can a training solution be implemented to fill these gaps in knowledge, skills, or attitude?

Beyond linking training to business strategy, training can be used as a business strategy in and of itself. A recent ASTD study of 575 publicly traded companies demonstrates that companies that spent the most on employee development outperformed those that spent the least (Bassi, Ludwig, McMurrer & Van Buren, 2001). ASTD concludes that those companies with the greatest increases in total stockholder returns between 1998 and 1999 reported higher levels of spending on training, measured both as a percentage of payroll and on a per-eligible-employee basis. Further, a study by Hackett Benchmarking and Research indicates that companies with a high investment in training experience lower levels of employee turnover.

Tied to Business and Performance Measures

Unless training and development professionals adjust their thinking about how training is measured, their training offerings will not help the organization meet its goals. Imagine, for example, a goal-setting workshop that participants rate favorably (level 1); participants' posttest scores are quite high (level 2); and the goal-setting skills are immediately implemented in the workplace (level 3). Despite these favorable results, there is no impact whatsoever on the organization as a whole (level 4). Yes, goal setting is nice, and the training was very effective at teaching individuals how to do it, but goal setting may not help the organization achieve its real objective of increasing market share by adding a new product line.

Of the companies surveyed in ASTD's benchmarking study and reported in the *2001 State of the Industry Report,* 77 percent conduct evaluations of participant reaction (level 1), but only 7 percent carry out level 4 evaluation based on return-on-investment (ROI) calculations (figure 3-1). Training and development professionals must shift from collecting reactive—and subjective—data after a program has been implemented to collecting data before, during, and after an intervention.

The first step is to reexamine how information is used from each evaluation level. For example, level 1 data should not be used to tout the achievements of a training function. Level 1 data is simply a feedback tool for the training function to address issues—such as program logistics—to improve program design and delivery, and, possibly, to cull marketing messages for the next time the program is offered.

Figure 3-1. Evaluation practices of ASTD's benchmarked companies.

Percentage of benchmarked companies who collect:

Level One Evaluation Data **77%**

Level Two Evaluation Data **38%**

Level Three Evaluation Data **14%**

Level Four Evaluation Data **7%**

0%   10%   20%   30%   40%   50%   60%   70%   80%

Source: Reprinted with permission from Van Buren, M.E. (2001). *State of the Industry Report 2001.* Alexandria, VA: ASTD.

Now the challenge is to think of new and more useful ways to evaluate training. The best way to approach evaluation is to establish baselines for certain measures prior to and at several intervals during and after training. These measures can be either "hard" data, such as units produced or error rate, or "soft" data, such as customer perception or morale. Extensive lists of hard and soft data units can be found in tables 3-2 and 3-3.

In addition, there may be measures of the general training function you might want to steadily collect. To remain consistent, you may wish to identify measures that are important to you and determine how excellence will be individually measured. Table 3-4 offers some examples.

Finally, once you have results to share, do so. Don't be bashful about tooting your own horn. You will build credibility for your products and services and enhance training's prestige in the organization as you market your successes. Stimulating demand for your services and finding appropriate learners for your interventions will cease to be a challenge.

One proven way to market your successes is to sell the positive results of a pilot initiative. In other words, instead of saying, "I've been reading about how important succession planning is, and I think our company ought to try something in this area," find a department experiencing pain in the area of succession and create a pilot project with them. Make sure that the project's results are applicable to a broad audience. Then, sell their positive results to other organizational departments.

Customer-Driven

In the 1980s, many companies decentralized training and development. In these forms, training representatives worked for the organizational units they served and reported not to an HR unit but to their unit's manager. This trend didn't last long.

Table 3-2. Examples of hard data.

Output	Time
Units produced	Equipment downtime
Tons manufactured	Overtime
Items assembled	On-time shipments
Money collected	Time to project completion
Items sold	Processing time
Forms processed	Supervisory time
Loans approved	Break-in time for new employees
Inventory turnover	Learning time
Patients visited	Meeting schedules
Applications processed	Repair time
Students graduated	Efficiency
Tasks completed	Work stoppages
Output per hour	Order response
Productivity	Late reporting
Work backlog	Lost-time days
Incentive bonus	
Shipments	**Quality**
New accounts generated	Scrap
	Waste
Costs	Rejects
Budget variances	Error rates
Unit costs	Rework
Cost by account	Shortages
Variable costs	Product defects
Fixed costs	Deviation from standard
Overhead cost	Product failures
Operating costs	Inventory adjustments
Number of cost reductions	Time-card corrections
Project cost savings	Percent of tasks completed properly
Accident costs	Number of accidents
Program costs	
Sales expense	

Source: Reprinted with permission from Phillips, J., and R.D. Stone. (2002). *How to Measure Training Success*. New York: McGraw-Hill Trade.

Today, training departments are predominantly centralized, with training professionals sharing resources, organizational structure, and insights. Although there are many virtues of a centralized training function, one clear danger is that training runs the risk of becoming an ivory tower—detached and isolated from the true problems of the organization.

If you are part of a centralized training organization, you must make every effort to remain connected to your organization. Visit the employees you serve and

Table 3-3. Examples of soft data.

Work Habits	Customer Service
Absenteeism	Customer complaints
Tardiness	Customer satisfaction
Visits to the dispensary	Customer dissatisfaction
First aid treatments	Customer impressions
Violations of safety rules	Customer loyalty
Number of communication breakdowns	Customer retention
Excessive breaks	Customer value
Follow-up	Lost customers
Work Climate and Job Satisfaction	**Employee Development and Advancement**
Number of grievances	
Number of discrimination charges	Number of promotions
Employee complaints	Number of pay increases
Job satisfaction	Number of learning programs attended
Employee turnover	Requests for transfer
Litigation	Performance appraisal ratings
Organizational commitment	Increases in job effectiveness
Employee loyalty	
Increased confidence	**Initiative and Innovation**
	Implementation of new ideas
	Successful completion of projects
	Number of suggestions implemented
	Setting goals and objectives
	New products and services developed
	New patents and copyrights

Source: Reprinted with permission from Phillips, J., and R.D. Stone. (2002). *How to Measure Training Success.* New York: McGraw-Hill Trade.

their supervisors often, if only to ask how things are going and find out what support people need. Even if their responses are not always training related, you will be closer to understanding your customer's problems, priorities, and strategies. This contact is one way of allowing employees and their managers to have a say in what training is conducted and how it is delivered. Periodic needs assessments—formal or informal—are a key marketing technique. Regular contact with your customer base is one of your key marketing tools, and it's easy to do.

Another way to facilitate shared responsibility for the direction of the training function is to establish a cross-departmental, mixed-level organizational training council. This group can help establish infrastructure for the training and development function, set policies, give input on training needs and projects, provide you with pilot audiences, share resources, market your programs, and more. Before

Table 3-4. Some general measures for the training function.

Measure	Rating
Percentage of employee population who participate in development (unique participants)	A = 50% or more B = 25% or more C = 10% or more D = Less than 10%
Number of different formats or delivery methods used for training	A = More than 10 B = 7–10 C = 5–6 D = 4 or fewer
Training budget as a percentage of the organization's overall operating expenses	A = Decreased B = Stayed the same C = Increased

starting such a committee, however, make sure that members understand the parameters in which they are working. Which decisions are theirs to make and which are outside their purview?

In the forum of a training council you will no doubt encounter some who are hostile to the concept of training and development. There will always be nay-sayers—regardless of the topic. It is important to give these individuals the opportunity to provide input into the training function, too. Encourage them to bring up any negative responses to proposed training efforts. You are bound to get these from other employees down the road and it helps you to formulate your responses. A good nay-sayer on a committee is valuable. You can also turn the tables on nay-sayers. When they ask, "How do I keep my department productive while I have to send my employees to training?" ask them, "How do you measure productivity?" Often these are the managers who won't know, or, who, when challenged, realize that they measure productivity by skills that your program intends to impart.

Accountability at All Levels

THE CEO LEVEL. Studies have shown that senior-level managers acting as advocates of corporate-wide learning efforts are the most powerful means of informing and inspiring others within the company.

Commitment from senior management, says Pennsylvania State University professor William J. Rothwell, "means that top managers not only say they want development efforts but are willing to back it up with personal participation and resources." Jeanne Meister (2001) details seven key roles CEOs can take on to back up their stated commitment to training:

1. *CEO as visionary:* Presents a clear direction for corporate learning around which the organization can rally
2. *CEO as sponsor:* Provides encouragement, resources, and commitment for strategic learning to flourish and develop; sponsors groundbreaking new learning programs
3. *CEO as governor:* Takes an active role in governing the corporate learning function, reviews goals and objectives, provides direction on how to measure the effectiveness of learning, and evaluates outcomes
4. *CEO as subject matter expert:* Actively takes on the role of thought leader and develops new learning programs for the entire organization
5. *CEO as teacher:* Teaches programs on site or provides resources to create online learning platforms that are used to deliver new enterprisewide learning programs
6. *CEO as learner:* Becomes the role model for lifelong learning for the entire organization and acknowledges his or her willingness to constantly learn
7. *CEO as chief marketing agent:* Promotes the company's commitment to learning by mentioning it in speeches, the annual report, press interviews, reports to security analysts, and general marketing tools such as posters, email messages, and articles in the company magazine.

In his role as "CEO as chief marketing agent," for example, General Electric Company's former CEO Jack Welch is known to have made public statements like this one: "An organization's ability to learn and translate that learning into action rapidly is the ultimate competitive advantage." And, as "CEO as governor," Michael Dell, CEO of Dell Computer Corporation, sent personal emails to all managers who were being required to take instruction on ethics and values, letting them know he expected 100 percent of managers to meet the requirement. He requested regular updates, detailing who was on track for completing the mandate. The heads of divisions that were falling behind got emails from him. Some got telephone calls. The few individuals not in compliance by the end of the year received personal notes. The 100 percent target was achieved.

To help your CEO take on these roles, you must keep your senior executives up-to-date about organizational learning activities. What's planned for the coming months? What are next year's planned activities? Publish an annual report for your training function. Share your business plan (which must be tied to the organization's business plan) with senior management regularly.

A Note From the City Manager

Redwood City is working very hard to be a learning organization. Training is but one method of learning. It is the responsibility of this organization to provide opportunities to all of you so you are able to develop your skills and reach your full potential. Continuous improvement and constant learning are basic themes of our city and are part of the culture. The city's responsibility is to make training available, and your responsibility is to make use of these opportunities. Please review the various training opportunities contained in this booklet. When we stop learning, we start dying.

Ed Everett, city manager, City of Redwood City

THE SUPERVISOR LEVEL. The supervisor has even more possible roles in employee development than does the CEO. The training function often has more leverage and effect when working at the supervisor level.

When supervisors are asked, "What is your role in employee development?" they answer in a wide range of ways: "to coach and mentor my employees," "to provide them with autonomy," "to encourage them to continuously develop themselves," "to give them time off to attend training," and "to make sure I budget for training expenses."

The supervisor's role in employee development is all these things and more. In their study of the successful implementation of e-learning, ASTD and the MASIE Center (2001) found that participants were unable to see the value of the course unless their managers:

- made clear why they should take course
- linked content to workplace and business objectives and future career opportunities
- displayed an interest in the course
- gave status and importance to participation
- provided context assignments and work samples to transfer to the reality of workplace
- assigned peers to provide support or dialogue.

Clearly, a good deal of a supervisor's job could be spent on employee development, and it is your job to make it easy for supervisors to do so. You must help managers understand their role in developing others. Management topics that might be included in your course catalog include mentoring and coaching and understanding your role in developing others. You might also wish to develop a guide for managers to help them appreciate and understand their role (appendix A).

You need to teach managers how to recognize when employees will benefit from training. For example, persistent quality problems or low employee morale may indicate an appropriate training opportunity. You need to help supervisors understand what training options they have, including different types of training. You also need to have systems, such as online tracking tools and individual development plans, in place to help managers track and observe the growth of their employees. You must help make employees personally accountable for their own learning by providing such tools as a learning contract that both the supervisor and the employee complete before embarking on a training intervention.

When marketing a specific training event to supervisors, include the objectives of the event, techniques to support the new learning, and ideas for integrating the participant's learning into their day-to-day functions. For example, the supervisor could invite the learner to speak at a staff meeting about the training; allow the learner to do individual, on-the-job training for other employees; or grant the learner a fresh job assignment that utilizes the new skills.

THE EMPLOYEE'S ROLE. How do we get learners accountable for their own training? According to Christine Bennett of WorkVantage, "Individual employees need the understanding and skills fundamental to self-accountability. They need to know who they are, where they plan to go, and what steps are required to get them there. In our business, we say the first step is to think of oneself as 'Me, Myself, and I, Inc.' Armed with learners who have clear, *self-determined* development goals, you have active participants in the planning, design, and delivery of training that matters."

According to Daniel Tobin (1998), the way to get employees to take responsibility for their own training is to make them responsible for their own career paths. He advises using a learning contract personalized for each employee and negotiated by the employee and his manager. The contract should include

- the company's business goals and how the employees' individual work contributes to their achievement
- how the employee's work must change to help the company achieve its goals
- what learning is needed in order to make those changes
- a learning plan, including a schedule and a list of necessary learning resources
- measures of learning achievement
- ways to apply the learning on the job
- changes in business results that may be expected from the application of the learning to the job.

One way to develop learner accountability is to integrate training plans and objectives in the performance evaluation process. Certification programs and standards for how many training hours employees need to complete are other methods to create accountability. But, both have their pitfalls (table 3-5).

Two other ways to involve employees in training initiatives are to teach people how to learn and to use employees as in-house workshop facilitators.

Hold classes for all employees on learning processes. Make sure employees know how to question information, how to break up ideas, how to tie learning to organizational goals, ways to accelerate learning, and so on.

Whenever possible, use in-house facilitators. Not only is this an economical option, but it adds credibility with your audience and helps develop the talents and skills of the employees chosen to facilitate the training. For example, let bilingual employees train other employees in their native language. Tom Tierney, managing director of Bain & Company (an international strategy consulting firm), is quoted as saying, "Our internal data shows us that our partners rank being a trainer as one of the most outstanding activities of their careers. I would never want to go to a cadre of professional trainers to do the bulk of our training. I want consultants, managers, and senior partners all involved in training. As trainers they learn more. They become more integrated and committed to the firm's goals and values. They come back from the programs truly energized. They show their student colleagues what it means to be a committed teacher-learner" (Meister, 2001).

Table 3-5. Pitfalls of certification programs and mandated training hours.

Potential Pitfalls When Creating Certification Programs	Potential Pitfalls When Establishing Standards of How Many Training Hours Employees Should Complete
• Requirements are not valid and reliable • You don't know how you'll measure achievement • No tracking system is in place • There are no clear rewards for completing the certificate • There is no link to a real career path • If there is a timeline for completion, it isn't realistic • There aren't clear, concise objectives that link to the organization's bottom line • Certification isn't really necessary; training itself would have sufficed	• Not everyone is aware of the standard and why you have one • There isn't a way to track training hours completed • There isn't a consequence for failing to meet the standard or a reward for completion • What counts toward the requirement is not clear (e.g., does a sales meeting count? a new product training? training that occurs outside the organization? degree programs?)

Training Anywhere and Everywhere

It is often hard to market training because people see it as a distraction from productive work. They think of training as an event—usually classroom based—that takes people away from the work that needs to be done. And, with instructor-led classroom training still representing 79.9 percent of the delivery mechanisms at surveyed companies in 1999, they are often correct.

Table 3-6 shows how training time was spent between classroom training and learning technologies at 43 organizations from multiple industries that were part of ASTD's benchmarking survey.

Table 3-6. Trends in training methods.

	Percentage in 1999	Percentage Projected for 2002
Instructor-Led Classroom	79.9	67.5
Learning Technologies	8.4	18.2

Source: Van Buren, M.E. (2001). *State of the Industry Report 2001*. Alexandria, VA: ASTD.

Several alternative formats for professional development were also used at the benchmarked companies, including tuition reimbursement, employer-supported conference attendance, rotational training staff (when nontraining employees are assigned training duties on a temporary basis), train-the-trainer courses, training resource center, apprenticeship training, mentoring or coaching programs, and mandatory annual training time (Van Buren, 2001).

Much of the industry buzz nowadays is about e-learning, but there continue to be effective methods of instruction that are neither classroom- nor computer-based. For example, Noontime University offers lunch hour training by telephone.

How I Think Outside the Classroom

I first thought that I do not partake of any development, but I've come to understand that classroom programs aren't the only way to learn. I admit that I've experienced some development, raising the question of where it came from. I think I've recognized the need to develop new responsibilities in a new role and jumped ship accordingly (three times now). I've also tried to look closely at those around me whose skills I found impressive in one or more respects.

Todd D. Rosentover, chief risk officer, First Equity Card Corporation

Training bulletins, job aids, and workbooks are still valid methods of imparting knowledge. Electronic performance support systems (EPSS) that teach skills on the equipment the employee is using are good examples of just-in-time learning. Job rotation and "stretch" assignments are workplace interventions that promote employees' professional growth. People start to see training as a job enhancement, not as a separate effort.

These training methods should complement each other, not replace each other. Blended approaches to learning are predicted to be most widely used in the next several years. For example, a leadership development program might have modules that are offered in the classroom, on-the-job, at the computer, and in reading materials. Blended approaches rely upon the best methods to impart each specific piece of content.

Utilization of a Fee-for-Service Model

There are some fee structures that organizations use to try to improve the effectiveness of training activities. Fee-for-service arrangements, for example, are based on the concept that training departments can be more responsive to departmental needs when they "contract" with the department for its business. The pros and cons to this approach are many and are summarized here by Paul Van Houten, director of training and OD at the department of human resources for the city and county of San Francisco. Van Houten's division provides consulting services, facilitation, and training programs for 60 departments and 30,000 employees on a fee-for-service model. According to Van Houten:

> The principal pro for this model is greater accountability on the part of the training and OD function. Training and OD interventions are focused on the clients. The goal is to serve as internal consultants and deliver a specific product, tailored to the department's needs. By so doing, unclear expectations are eliminated up front. In addition, one must constantly streamline one's services to become a more efficient operating group.
>
> The cons of this approach include the fact that charging a fee may discourage some departments from participating in the program because they can't afford it. Smaller departments can band together to pay for a shared program. Sometimes we are pressed to move on to the next project quickly, leaving minimal time to debrief a project or to incorporate fully the lessons learned from the experience. It is important to resist the pressure to move on without allowing time for reflection and learning.
>
> Another con is that there is a large amount of overhead or support work to complete—tracking, billing, collections, and reports. After all, departments want to know what they are paying for. Finally, clients sometimes come to the training and development function with a preconceived direction; they have a

particular problem or issue they want to address and think training is the answer. We risk losing their business if we suggest a different organizational response that we believe will be more effective. The point is to provide effective, efficient services that deliver a product that truly meets the client's needs.

Some fee models that seem at first to encourage participation in training events may actually have the opposite effect in the long term. For example, consider the use of no-show fees. With this fee model, when individuals who are registered for classroom programs do not attend, their departments are charged. Although there is some good logic behind this fee—managers will be motivated to release their employee so that the department doesn't incur a charge, no-shows don't take spots away from others in popular classes, and your department doesn't incur the costs of an additional participant—this is actually a fee for "nonservice" and has a significant downside. That is, to avoid the no-show fee, managers will often send someone else in the place of the previously registered employee who is unable to attend. The problem is that this employee may not have a need or desire for learning about the topic. This leads to an unfavorable perception of training by this individual as well as of his or her fellow participants who suffer the consequences of the diluted audience makeup.

* * *

The ideas promoted in this chapter are not ideas that can happen overnight and are not ideas that any individual can institute on his or her own. If you work for a training function that is a centralized, stand-alone endeavor that is funded annually and prefers traditional classroom formats, it doesn't mean that you are doomed to failure or that your marketing won't work. It just makes your job of promoting development more of a struggle than you should have to contend with.

 Now What?

With what ideas or actionable ideas should you walk away from this chapter?

- Creating a workplace that has seen and understood the value of development is your best marketing tool.
- Seek ways to make the shift to a training function that is
  — integrated into organizational systems and strategic initiatives
  — driven by business strategy and customer needs
  — tied to business and performance measures

— creating accountability among individuals at all levels in the organization for developmental activities

— customer-driven

— continuously utilizing nontraditional delivery methods

— utilizing a fee-for-service or other funding structure that makes training accountable to its various customer bases.

Chapter Four

Addressing Motivation: **Your Buyers'**

****

 ## **A Quick Look**

Marketers of training products and services could constantly call upon prospective clients hawking their wares, but that type of marketing doesn't appeal to today's buyer. Additionally, it's not any fun for the marketer, and it doesn't yield great results. The best way for a provider of training and development products or services to market is to build relationships. When providers have strong relationships with clients, clients want to hire providers when the right opportunity comes along. And it's not just external consultants who have clients. As internals read this chapter, keep in mind that, unless you aren't accountable to anyone organizationally, you, too, have to build these types of relationships.

Chapter **Features**

* Eleven traits of successful training suppliers and seven characteristics of good clients
* Principles of permission marketing that can be utilized by internals and externals alike
* Internal and external fee negotiation
* What turns an internal buyer off?
* Competencies addressed:
  — Relationship building
  —Comprehending organizational and individual behavior
  — Analysis
  — Questioning techniques

Do you interrupt your prospective clients, or do you invite them to talk when they're ready? Have you "dated" your clients before asking them to "get married"? The focus of traditional marketing has been promoting products or services to audiences who may or may not be ready to take in the information. The focus of more contemporary marketing is building relationships—finding out what your prospective audience members need and exposing them to how you can help them to meet those needs. Relationship building takes time and effort, but the result is that you don't have to take on the role of a door-to-door salesperson. When your prospective clients come across the right opportunity, they'll want to hire you.

Building Relationships With Your Customers

Whether you are an external training provider or an internal one, you have customers. Internal trainers need to focus on relationship building with the sponsors of their programs as much as externals do. After all, you may not see yourself as being in direct competition with an external vendor, but you are (Scott, 2000). Although this chapter focuses primarily on the external supplier-internal client relationship, the relationship-building ideas are equally applicable to the internal provider and the internal customer.

What is this idea of building relationships? Seth Godin, founder and CEO of Yoyodyne, the industry's leading interactive direct marketing company, revolutionized the field of marketing with the model he advanced in his book *Permission Marketing* (1999). The basic premise of Godin's approach is that instead of relying on what he calls "interruption marketing" techniques used in the past, whereby marketers had to interrupt people's lives with their marketing messages (at the same time that millions of other marketers were doing the same thing), marketers should instead ask permission to provide information on buyers' schedules and at their request.

Godin compares interruption marketing to walking up to someone in a crowded, noisy bar and asking him or her to get married. If that person turns you down, you move on to another one until you find someone, possibly, who will say yes. A permission marketer, he says, "goes on a date. If it goes well, the two of them go on another date. And then another. Until, after ten or twelve dates, both sides can really communicate with each other about their needs and desires. After twenty dates they meet each other's families. Finally, after three or four months of dating, the permission marketer proposes marriage."

What ensures that external providers get past the first few dates with their internal prospects? What makes the internal provider of training and development services the provider of choice for organizations? Successful relationships are built when marketers

1. *Have passion about their products or services:* Passion is infectious and helps clients get excited about your work, too.
2. *Ask questions:* Good marketers spend more time asking questions and listening to the responses than they do promoting themselves or their offerings.
3. *Understand the audience's, the organization's, and the client's needs:* When you understand the circumstances in which clients, or client companies, find themselves, they know that what you provide them will be a good fit.
4. *Provide instructionally sound offerings:* Your products and services must be designed to be engaging, and they must effectively utilize principles of adult learning.
5. *Have expertise buyers lack:* Whether it's knowledge of particular subject matter or a new medium for imparting the subject matter, you must have the edge on your buyers.
6. *Have resources buyers don't:* You need access to resources that span the gamut from technology to human resources to time.
7. *Have star power:* If you call, clients accept your calls. If you don't call, they seek you out.
8. *Come with strong references:* People clients admire tell them how happy they are with your products or services.
9. *Provide demonstrations:* For many individuals, a hands-on trial is the only way for them to envision what you can do.
10. *Provide excellent customer service and follow-up:* You are responsive, friendly, and professional.
11. *Are well connected to people and ideas:* Clients know that if you cannot help them that you will refer them to someone else who can, and you often share what you pick up from your external network with your individual clients.

A Closer Look at Relationship-Building Principles

The following sections describe more clearly how these factors play out when you are trying to build a solid relationship with a new or prospective customer.

1. HAVE PASSION. What will win a potential client over is not a complete listing of your capabilities or past experiences. It is not a glossy brochure. It is not even, necessarily, a stunning product. It is passion—your enthusiasm, energy, and deep belief in what you have to offer. The good news for training and development professionals, then, is that you don't have to be a salesperson. You just need to share your passion, and you'll have a customer as eager to use your services as you are to provide them.

> **Why I Buy**
>
> If you cannot muster up enthusiasm or are unwilling to share your passion about your work with me, why then would I be interested in hiring you? Where is my incentive? Look at marketing as sharing your passion about something you love and are great at. People buy other people as opposed to services. It is a proven fact of sales. I choose my dentist, accountant, and most other services I buy, not only by someone's competency, but by how they present to me, how passionate they are about their work, and how happy they seem being engaged in it. After all, I am never going to have much energy for dental or accounting work, but I sure expect the people I hire to.
>
> **Nance Cheifetz,** corporate fairy godmother, A Sense of Delight

2. ASK QUESTIONS. Remember how on your first dates you asked the other person to tell you a little bit about himself or herself? One of the best ways to build a relationship is to ask questions and listen to the responses. For you, these questions include the following:

- What are employee needs?
- What organizational issue prompted the request for training?
- What is the business plan for your department?
- What is the goal you are trying to achieve?
- What is it that you liked or disliked about suppliers you have used in the past?
- How are learners likely to respond to this initiative?

You also need two other important pieces of information about the client to help you market your training. You must ask, "How long have you been a training manager (or whatever the client's role is)?" and "How do you typically work with consultants?"

Think about it: If you were selling knee braces for athletes, would you make the same marketing pitch to an athlete who's played the sport for eight years as to an athlete who's played it for eight days? The newer athlete, who's fresh but less experienced, doesn't necessarily know how hard the play will be on his knees. The more experienced player may have already been injured, has probably already tried other types of braces, and knows what he is looking for. A one-size-fits-all approach won't work with individuals who have different experiences and different motivators for purchasing.

The same is true of training managers. More experienced managers have made hiring mistakes. They've tried plenty of other suppliers in the past so they know what they are looking for. They also have different goals. Experienced managers struggle with questions like these: "How can I make this training really effective? How can I show its bottom-line effects to the organization? How can I ensure my employees are still using it months down the road?" This questioning attitude is very different from that of a new, less experienced trainer who is likely to be more responsive to training requests made by someone more senior. If they've been asked to provide diversity training, they want to provide the best diversity training possible so that they can build credibility. They less often push back or challenge the request.

An excellent, but widely overlooked question to ask in your initial conversations with potential clients is, "How do you typically work with consultants (or suppliers)?" Wouldn't answers like these be useful to you as a consultant?

- "I use 'shadow consultants,' people whose skills are more advanced than mine who can act as a behind-the-scenes advisor."
- "We bring in consultants to design and develop all of our programs and then train our trainers to deliver them."
- "I develop meeting or retreat agendas for our senior leadership and hire a facilitator to lead them."

How Do I Usually Work With Consultants?

Before exploring external training options, we exhaust our internal resources. Especially in today's economy, we turn first to "resident experts" and find ways to share resources. We also pay a monthly fee to a program in St. Louis called BizLibrary that allows us to check out up to two videos or programs at a time. Only when we have a large number of employees who require training on a subject (20 in our case) and the training is mission critical, do we bring in outsiders. If it's considered fluff or a soft-skill subject, such as customer service training, we usually conduct the training ourselves rather than bring in a professional.

We are primarily interested in Web-based training and follow-up online materials after training to minimize the expense of having a trainer come in once, provide a class, and leave us with materials that become outdated, sometimes in as little as a few months. Everyone has a different schedule so what works best is flexible, computer-based information with short visits from live trainers to make the materials come to life.

Rebecca Linquist, training manager, REInfoLink

3. Understand the Audience's, the Organization's, and the Client's Needs. Buyers will find it much easier to trust you when you demonstrate that you understand the needs of their audiences or organizations. Among other things, buyers want to see that you and your product are a good match with the culture or learning style of the potential audience. They want you to be able to relate to the employees to whom your services are to be marketed—whether they are custodians or the chief information officer. They'll be able to measure the fit by the language that you use and by the examples that you provide.

As an outsider, one can often contribute a unique insight on an organization's needs. You have access to research, company or competitor data, and trends that buyers might not be aware of.

4. Provide Offerings That Are Instructionally Sound. Marketing training programs to line managers or to individuals who are not trainers by trade can seem almost easier than marketing to folks knowledgeable about the field. When marketing to other training professionals, you need to understand the principles of instructional design, and you must make sure your products and services are instructionally sound. If you aren't yet familiar with instructional design concepts, pick up some of the books in the Additional Resources section of this book. If you don't ground your offerings in good instructional design principles and principles of adult learning, you won't get far with a good client.

These days, most buyers want to see a balance of academics (theory) and practicality in the content you deliver. Especially with technologically based training interventions, buyers need to see that your program is instructionally sound and not just bells and whistles.

5. Have Expertise Buyers Lack. Although organizations amass great deals of collective knowledge, there are going to be certain areas in which individuals in your client's company are just not subject matter experts. Or, they may have the knowledge but not the ability or the confidence to impart that knowledge to others.

Their need for expertise is your opportunity. If you do not have the expertise yourself, you can develop a stable of consultant experts who do. What's important is that your clients know that you are the person who can meet their need for expertise.

6. Have Resources Clients Don't. Maybe the client does have the subject matter expertise but simply doesn't have the time to develop a related training intervention. Maybe the client has done the development but doesn't have the means (or techniques) to distribute the idea organizationally. Maybe the client doesn't have human resources to help develop or execute the project. Maybe they don't have the technology to put their tried-and-true classroom program into a computer-based format. It may even be something as simple as their lack of useable training space or a computer laboratory. Sometimes the people who most need your services have the least time to weed through their resources or even to bring you in for a meeting to talk about their challenges.

As an outsider, you often don't operate under the same constraints as the internal purchaser (though you surely have plenty of your own!). When you are not hampered by the same staffing, political, or time constraints as your potential clients, you appeal to those who appreciate action and efficiency.

7. Have Star Power. According to Alan Weiss (1992), "If you are dependent on seeking out prospects and convincing each one to buy your services, you are limited by the amount of time in a day. If prospects are dependent on seeking you out to secure your assistance, you are limited by the amount of growth you are willing to accept." Make your name, firm, and talents known, and get prospective clients to call you. Get organizationally, locally, or even nationally and internationally famous by

- writing newsletter or magazine articles, book chapters, or entire books
- speaking at conferences, trade shows, and association meetings
- appearing on television or speaking on the radio
- having an Internet presence
- being listed in professional directories, referral services, or chamber of commerce listings.

8. Come With Strong References. One thing that can minimize the buyer's work screening you as a potential vendors is when someone he or she admires has already used your services or products. This is why the practice of asking your satisfied customers to recommend you to their friends and colleagues is one of the most effective marketing tools you have.

9. Provide Demonstrations. Which Sunday morning newspaper insert are you more likely to open—the one that is an ad for a new line of skin care products or the one that is an ad and contains sample skin care products? Many marketers are banking on your use of the samples. They hope you'll use them, like them, continue to use them, and tell your friends about it. Although this particular type of sampling is more of an interruption marketing technique (as it is sent blindly to individuals unsolicited), offering previews to those qualified candidates who want one is a surefire success.

David Parks of tompeterscompany! sees previews as opportunities to help buyers make informed decisions about whether his company's interventions are the right vehicles to fix problems at the client company. These events are not sales pitches, he stresses, but opportunities to give clients insight about what their workshops are about, to provide a feel for the quality of their trainers, and to provide some experiential learning through a microcosm of training. His free online seminars (marketed solely on their Website and via email) netted 8,000 registrations in six months. Even with a 50 percent dropout rate for these "Webinars," that still leaves 4,000 people who have heard the company's message in the six-month period. Even if your product isn't as tangible as a seminar, even your pro bono attendance at a project planning meeting gives clients a sample of what it's like to work with you and what type of ideas and experience you bring to the table.

Previews are essential for those buyers who are less intuitive and more tactile and need to see or touch something to help them understand how it will work. Offer previews so that this sometimes heard complaint isn't said about you, "I know that they could do something great for us, I just have no idea what it would be."

10. PROVIDE EXCELLENT CUSTOMER SERVICE AND FOLLOW-UP. Certainly customers expect the basics of exceptional service—timely response to their calls, professionalism, follow-through on your promises, and courtesy. They want to be communicated with in the format that they prefer. Find out if that is via phone, email, fax, or some other means of communication.

Many consulting manuals recommend being in contact with your client base (past, current, and potential) once a month. How can you establish some credible basis to connect with your client on that frequent a schedule? Here are some ideas, but don't stretch it:

- send an announcement about or copies of articles you've written (on any topic)
- forward articles you've found related to what you have spoken about with the client
- describe any new products or services you offer
- send your own newsletter
- send gifts especially around holidays
- pass along cartoons or photographs
- describe results you've achieved elsewhere or a summary of results you've achieved for the client.

If you really don't have any reason for contacting the client, then don't make something up. The client can tell, and it's a waste of everyone's time.

Exceptional service and monthly contact are the essentials of maintaining your client relationships. But, what makes you even more desirable as a partner is going beyond these basics. For example, if you offer services that can take some of the logistical work off the customer's plate (course registrations, room reservations, evaluation analysis, even marketing), you'll be appreciated. Not only do these valuable services help the client, they help you, too. If the client drops the ball on your project, it will not be used and will likely fail.

Why I Buy

I contracted with our online learning provider for our corporate university for a number of reasons. The quality of the course content was excellent. The information was solid and well presented in an interactive format. They had a large variety of course offerings. From technical training to soft skills, employees could choose from hundreds of titles. They provided a built-in marketing plan with a compact disc that contained fliers and newsletter articles we could use to promote the e-learning initiative. The provider's customer service is great. They return calls immediately, they always sound happy to hear from me, even when things are in chaos. The technical support is also superb. They "walk" you through the problem, explain things in an understandable way, and provide great follow-up. And, their reputation was excellent. They'd been in the business for a number of years, have won several big awards, and provided great references.

Carol Gifford, employee development analyst, city of Westminster, Colorado

---

11. ARE WELL CONNECTED TO PEOPLE AND IDEAS. Being a good networker is a good marketing skill, good business practice, and a selling point for potential clients. It's been proven repeatedly that letting everyone you know know what you do can lead to potential assignments. Networking can help you find out, for example, who is using outside providers, who is sending out requests for bids (and how to get on the list of bidders), and who is hiring training and development practitioners and might need assistance in the interim.

Having a network of people who do work similar to yours is a business asset when you are too busy to take on another client project, when you need feedback on something you'd rather not yet share with a client, or when you need to quickly assemble a client team. In addition, when you share resources and ideas from your network with your client, you add additional value.

A proven networking method is membership in related professional associations. You'll be exposed to key players and innovative ideas, learn the jargon, and get exposure for your services. Just joining professional associations so that you can list them on your résumé is not using your membership to its full avail. Consider the membership for the investment it is, and focus on achieving the maximum result of your investment by getting involved.

Myth: You get jobs simply by being in the right place at the right time.

Fact: There's always a story circulating about some consultant who was hired because he just happened to call and offer a service at exactly the moment that the buyer was looking for that service. This is not a marketing method to rely on, however, as it is based entirely on luck. What makes sense, however, is employing several of the ideas already presented to increase your chances of being in the right place at the right time.

Relationships occur between two (or more) parties. So far in this chapter, you have been exposed only to what makes an external training vendor successful. To rectify this one-sided perspective, Marty Brounstein, principal of the Practical Solutions Group and author of five management books, including his latest, *Managing Teams for Dummies,* offers these characteristics of a promising client. According to Brounstein (2002), a good client

- *has a strong handle on the training needs of his or her targeted audience:* They want to have, and work to have, a pulse on the learning needs of their employee population. If a needs assessment is useful to determine fully the needs, good clients either handle it themselves or have a neutral party conduct it and work with him or her to analyze the results after it's done.
- *assists in course design:* They take an active interest in assisting in the course development process. They meet with external trainers in advance to get on board with the training plan and the content and activities that will be included. Good clients don't try to tell external trainers how to teach their courses but instead give the trainers insight so they can teach and challenge the group to learn effectively. They help customize case studies or other learning activities to make them relevant to the group.
- *thinks programs, not just classes:* Effective internal coordinators understand when a one-shot training is not going to produce the results they are seeking. They are willing to consider or contract for a series of learning sessions or modules over a period of time. They also talk about some kind of follow-up effort to help reinforce the learning and to build accountability among the participants.

- *sells assertively:* Good internal coordinators are positive, confident, and straightforward as they make their case for training with the decision makers in their organizations. In particular, they consider a training program more as an investment in development than as just a cost and usually have done a preliminary cost-benefit analysis to demonstrate how the training is something affordable and worthwhile to do. They are willing to start on a smaller scale, such as pilot groups, as a way to let the training sell itself. Finally, they promote training programs in a timely manner. They follow up fliers and email announcements with personal encouragement for learner involvement.

- *is action oriented:* Effective internal coordinators take a make-it-happen approach to getting training organized and implemented. They don't take weeks and months to get something done. They're responsive when you call, communicate continually, and follow through on what they said they would do.

- *gets the details handled:* Good internal coordinators handle the details of a training program quite well. Whether they do this work directly or through their support staff, everything is organized when the training begins. The facility is in order, the food is on hand, and the training materials are ready. Participants know when and where to come.

- *shows support:* Internal coordinators who do a good job care about the training and want it to be successful. As a result, they're quite supportive of your efforts. In addition, if the training is relevant for their position, they participate in the training. Such involvement gives the program a boost of support. It's leadership by example and makes that person's job of reinforcing the training afterward much more effective because of his or her direct participation. Support for the training also comes in the forms of timely feedback, heads-up communication on issues to be aware of, expression of appreciation, and just an interested inquiry on how the training is going with the group. These signs of care and concern for the trainer and the training program go a long way in making the external's job a whole lot easier.

A Critical Decision Factor: Cost

The primary difference between the relationship between an external provider and an internal buyer from a relationship between an internal provider and an internal customer is the fact that the external provider is paid directly by the internal buyer. Many people are very uncomfortable with this aspect of the relationship, from the inevitable question at a client meeting, "How much do you have budgeted for this?" or "How much will this cost?" to running into additional expenses along the way. Here are some tips to make the cost factor easier on both parties.

You don't want to establish prices that are too low. It can damage your credibility as buyers ponder why you are priced so far below your competitors. You also don't want to price yourself out of the market. It can be difficult, though, to find that perfect price point when ASTD reports wide price ranges for consultants: from $55 to $150 per hour, or $250 to $10,000 per day.

The second thing external providers must do is to recognize when they can negotiate on price in order to retain (or get) the business. If you decide that you want to work with a client, there are several ways to negotiate fees that create a win-win scenario. Here are some of them:

- Offer to bill the client in installments that straddle fiscal years.
- Offer a 10 percent discount when they pay on signing up, instead of after the service has been provided.
- Give discounts when they buy in bulk. For example, charge less than your daily rate when they contract for multiple days. Provide more than one program in a day or back-to-back services for a whole week.
- Let the client be your beta-pilot client. In return for the client's considered feedback and referrals, charge them only a minimal fee.
- Let clients host sessions that you can offer to the public. The client handles all the coordination internally and pays a small fee for the program, and you also market the program to your external contacts or to the local media to use the event as a showcase.
- Train remotely from your site. Use local video teleconferencing services to avoid travel costs.
- Offer clients several alternatives when you submit a proposal, or present fees "cafeteria style," allowing them to pick and choose training components that meet their needs within their budgetary constraints.
- Contribute some of your consulting fees to a nonprofit part of the organization. For example, Nancy Miller, "clutterologist," offers the City of Redwood City seminars on time and desk management and donates 10 percent of her fees to the Redwood City Public Library fund.
- Base your fees on value provided, not on your time or the tasks you'll perform.
- Allow the client to copy the program materials for you, or order them directly through Amazon.com instead of paying a high materials fee.
- Give a price discount for introductions to the client's network.
- Quote a reduced rate to get your foot in the door.

Barriers to Buying

What prevents individuals from buying? The number one factor cited in ASTD's *State of the Industry Report 2001* (Van Buren, 2001) for the decreasing percentage of payroll spent on outside training companies is the desire to maintain control over content. Other de-motivators are the flipsides of the motivators previously described: You don't show your passion, meet a need, or have resources the buyer doesn't already have. Additionally, you might just inadvertently hit one of the client's hot buttons.

What turns the client off when an external provider calls? The answer may be found in the following round-up of opinions from 20 internal buyers:

- "When they alienate my staff. My staff is my support system and deserves respect. If you don't respect them, then how will you respect the target audience for your products? Additionally, I then have to convince others of why I should use you and risk having my judgment questioned."
- "When they get my name wrong—repeatedly!"
- "Even though I don't see myself as a status seeker, I do get annoyed when vendors talk to me as if I am some peon, when they don't know my level in the organization."
- "Badmouthing the competition just shows lousy sportsmanship. And, if I've already used or hired a competitor and the provider I'm working with makes degrading comments about them, then they are questioning my judgment and I don't appreciate that. I'd rather they have knowledge of what their competitors do and what they charge and that they can then tell me what is different about the services each company provides."
- "When they hound me, like the company that sent me a video to review and then called six times to find out if I'd viewed it yet."
- "The hard sell."
- "When they say, 'This is easy' or 'I did this exact thing for another client.' I know they mean to say, 'I can handle this,' or 'I have relevant experience I can put to use,' but it sometimes feels like they're saying, 'What you do for a living is simple' or 'You're going to get a cookie cutter solution.'"

Who Holds the Purse Strings?

One of these turn-offs stems from the situation where the external party doesn't know who has buying power in the organization. You can get by without knowing this; your direct mail will probably get forwarded to that person eventually anyway. One approach is to "aim high." If you address an inquiry to a higher level official, you could hit the mark and discover he or she is indeed the buyer, or the higher-up can pass your inquiry down to a direct report who would not be in the least offended by receiving mail that was actually addressed to the boss. Or, you could take the holistic approach that everyone is a potential buyer—from the audience you intend to reach to their supervisors to senior management. But, knowing who can make the buying decision will save you time and energy and help you make a more professional impression.

Galvin (2001) concludes in *Training* magazine's "2001 Industry Report" that the training/HR department dominates the lion's share, or 61 percent, of training purchases. Sixteen percent is purchased by the individual trainee's department, 13 percent by the IT department, and 6 percent by the individual trainee. Also, the HR and IT departments control more than 81 percent of IT training purchases.

But, what if you're sitting in a meeting with a potential client and want to find out if he or she specifically has buying authority? Although this shouldn't be the first question you ask, if you are getting close to a sale, you can ask questions like these that probe organizational boundaries and attempt to get at who has what authority:

- What are your job responsibilities?
- How do you divvy up the work of this department? (Or, may I see an organizational chart?)
- What projects have you sponsored in the past?
- What is the process for making an investment of this sort?
- Is this the kind of organization where there is an emphasis on group buy-in, or do certain departments make decisions?

News that marketing your training and development products is really just about creating positive relationships—whether that's an external-internal or an internal-internal one—should come as a relief to many training providers who would prefer to focus on what they do than on having to sell it.

Now What?

With what ideas or actionable ideas should you walk away from this chapter?

- Uncover the potential buyer's needs, and then discuss with them only what you can do or provide that fits the buyer's circumstances.
- Sell your passion, not a laundry list of your capabilities.
- Practice permission marketing by inviting potential buyers to ask you to tell them more at a time when they need or want to.

- Ask yourself these key questions to capitalize on buyer motivation:
  — Do you have passion about your products or services?
  — Do you have strong relationships with potential buyers?
  — Do you understand the buyer's needs and the buyer's organization's needs?
  — Do your offerings adhere to principles of adult learning and sound instructional design?
  — Do you have an area of expertise?
  — What resources do you bring to the table?
  — Do you have star power?
  — Do you have glowing references to provide?
  — Can you offer a demonstration or preview?
  — Is your customer service top-notch?
  — Do you have monthly contact with clients or potential clients?
  — Are you networked?
- Two good questions to ask are how long have you been a training manager and how do you usually work with consultants.
- Establish prices that are neither too high nor too low, and enlist the client's help in creating win-win cost-saving ideas.

Section Two

Marketing Nuts and Bolts

✳✳✳

To be successful, training professionals need to employ skills used by professionals in the field of marketing. Section two highlights some of the marketing skills that weren't necessarily covered during our own professional training.

The chapters in this section address competencies in project planning, written and verbal expression, and graphic design, with a healthy dose of creativity thrown in. They are

* Chapter 5: Building the Campaign
* Chapter 6: Building on Your Success
* Chapter 7: How to Write Like a Marketer
* Chapter 8: How to Format Like a Graphic Designer.

You can use all the tips and techniques provided in chapters 5 through 8 as you are performing the usual tasks involved in creating and disseminating training and development initiatives. To mount a successful marketing campaign doesn't necessarily take a great deal of extra time, just a few new ideas and skills found here.

Chapter Five

Building the Campaign

✳✳

 ## A **Quick** Look

You've now focused on what motivates learners and buyers to invest in development. Now how do you transform their good intentions into action? This is achieved through a marketing campaign. A marketing campaign is a project plan for accomplishing tasks related to promoting your products and services. The tasks in the marketing plan include establishing objectives, choosing marketing strategies to achieve them, testing, measuring, and adapting. The beauty of this process is that it dovetails perfectly with the curriculum design process. Incorporating these marketing tasks into the project planning you are already engaged in will help you establish buy-in and locate appropriate participants for your learning opportunities.

Chapter **Features**

* Seven tasks in a marketing campaign
* Fifty ways to market
* When to work with an internal marketing department or an external marketing firm
* Checklist for hiring a marketing firm
* Marketing competencies addressed:
  — Project planning
  — Relationship building
  — Creativity

What Is a Marketing Campaign?

It requires a concentrated effort to convert motivation into action. That is your marketing campaign. You need a plan to create a desired response among a set of predefined customers. For example, for the marketing department at an automotive company that sells minivans, the set of customers might be young mothers. The desired response might be to take a test drive. For a marketer of internal training, the target audience might be employees who work at the front desk, and the desired behavior might be to register for an upcoming conference on the essentials of front desk management. For a marketer of external products and services, the audience might be senior management at insurance companies, and the desired response might be to fill out a survey on succession planning that can be used by the external provider to prepare an industrywide report.

When Do You Need to Create a Marketing Plan?

You'll need a marketing plan when you are embarking on a new project and are completing a project plan. Anytime you are involved in project planning, you will need to factor in marketing tasks like the ones previously described. When you fail to do so, your project may suffer from lack of buy-in and, later, from lack of participation in your initiative.

Additionally, a marketing plan is necessary when you have a new product or service to introduce. Failing to create a marketing campaign when you have a new product or service will make it less likely that you will find an appropriate audience or that you will expose the right people to your product or service.

Finally, marketing plans are instrumental for promoting events. When you perform the tasks that are part of a marketing campaign, you can be sure that the maximum number of appropriate people will take advantage of the learning opportunity you are providing. If you don't adhere to a marketing campaign, you risk losing your target audience, no matter how relevant your project is to your target audience's needs or how brilliant the content.

How Might Your Marketing Campaign Look?

Just as there is no single model for curriculum design, there is no single model of how to market one's products or services. Regardless of how these tasks are ordered or named, these are the key components of a marketing strategy:

1. *Define your target audience:* Whom do you want to reach? Who is the best user of your product or service? Who would respond to your offerings most favorably?
2. *Research your target audience's preferences and motivation:* What drives your target audience? What are the demographics of that audience, including its potential size?
3. *Establish marketing objectives:* What action do you want members of your target audience to take when they experience your marketing campaign?
4. *Choose a marketing strategy to achieve objectives:* Which marketing strategy will work best with your audience—posters on office bulletin boards or free mouse pads? What message is best? What look is best? What will be the frequency and reach of your marketing efforts?
5. *Test out the selected strategy on your target audience:* Roll out the marketing strategy.
6. *Measure:* How does the audience react? What changes need to be made to your marketing, or to your products and services based on the audience's reaction?
7. *Adapt:* What changes need to be made to your marketing, or to your products and services based on the audience's reaction?

You don't need to perform these seven steps discretely in an entirely separate and time-intensive marketing campaign. Table 5-1 shows how you can fit the seven steps of a marketing campaign into your training and development tasks.

The Marketing Campaign: Step by Step

1. Define Your Target Audience

Often, internal trainers will have their target audience prescribed to them. For example, they might be asked to "Offer a class on effective business writing for all company managers." A knowledge of marketing might help these internal trainers raise questions about the appropriateness of the identified group.

Table 5-1. Fitting a marketing campaign into your curriculum design process.	
Task in the Curriculum Design Process	**Where to Integrate the Curriculum Design Task in Your Marketing Campaign**
—	*Marketing Task 1:* Define your target audience, unless it is prescribed for you, in which case, skip this step.
Analysis: Explore request for training and the business need, ask key players their goals and expectations, create an audience profile, establish what content to cover, write project plan.	*Marketing Task 2:* Research your target audience's preferences and motivation.
Project Planning: Determine when and how you will bring your product or service to your participants, from analysis through evaluation and maintenance.	When you are doing your overall project planning, don't forget to include *Marketing Task 3:* Establish your marketing objectives.
Design: Write program objectives and course outline; create high-level design document; select formats, activities.	—
Development: Sit down and create materials, facilitators' guides, and so forth.	*Marketing Task 4:* Choose a marketing strategy.
Pilot: Try it out on the target audience.	*Marketing Task 5:* Test by putting initial marketing strategies out.
Delivery: Roll out the initiative.	*Marketing Task 6:* Measure by asking questions of participants and by tracking response rates and other key indicators of marketing effectiveness.
Evaluation and Maintenance: Measure effectiveness of the training and make changes to enhance the training.	*Marketing Task 7:* Adapt your marketing strategies as needed.

These trainers might be able to push back to help the organization determine what audience is really best for the given initiative. For example, is your business writing workshop geared at a specific level in the organization, a specific department, or an individual with specific characteristics: "Business Writing for Supervisors," "Business Writing for Research and Development," or "Business Writing for Individuals for Whom English Is a Second Language." This decision shouldn't be based on a whim, neither should it be based on which audience would be easiest to reach. Rather, it should be based on who would profit the most from the program, whose participation would most benefit the organization, and whose involvement in the program would help promote it further. Even if your audience is prescribed, it doesn't hurt to consider these questions if only to help you prepare for possible participant resistance or inappropriate learners in your interventions.

Another example is a leadership program offered to all organizational leaders as opposed to only those leaders who display high potential or top performance. Why is the latter a better audience? It is because they have the potential to make a greater positive impact on the organization. If you train mediocre leaders and bring them up to a level of good, they won't be able to do nearly as much good for the company as when you take great leaders and make them stellar.

External trainers can identify a market by function, by industry, or by some other characteristic. You can market your new training tracking software, for example, to "Lone Rangers" (training departments of one) who would appreciate one less administrative function on their plates, or you might decide it's best for the medical field in which there are extensive annual training requirements to track. Or, you may wish to market it to people who are already using a competitor's product that you know to be inferior to your organization's. This decision should also be based on who would most benefit from the program and whose participation in the program would best promote it, as well as the potential number of individuals you can reach.

2. Research Your Target Audience's Preferences and Motivation

What drives your target audience? For example, would "lightening my work load" be the key motivator for your "Lone Ranger" or for your supervisor audience? How many employees in the medical field are there in your geographic marketplace, and what is lacking in the tracking software they are currently using? In addition to asking how participants are likely to respond to the training and what their past experience with the topic has been, ask questions like the ones listed in table 5-2.

3. Establish Marketing Objectives

Objectives for marketing are important for the same reason that setting objectives for training is important: They help you define what you want to achieve, they focus your efforts, and it's the only way to know after the fact if your marketing campaign has been effective.

What is your marketing objective? Is it to have a company hire you to deliver a classroom program? Or, is it to get 30 participants to attend your next workshop? Perhaps your objective is to provide training to a targeted 20 percent segment of your employee population, or it may be to get all employees motivated to attend a mandated training program. Maybe you wish to ensure that all employees know

Table 5-2. Uncovering your target audience's motivations.

Motivation	Department
Size of target audience:	Level:
Benefits to this audience:	Age, experience, and background:
Work location (address):	Reading level:
Workspace characteristics:	Preferred communication format:
Tools used on the job:	Access to computer, telephone, and media:

how to access your online course catalog or motivate employees to attend an external conference? Maybe your objective is to grow your business by 20 percent?

Table 5-3 presents a simple model for marketing objectives. It's simple because it consists of only four parts, and because it is similar to the *ABCD* approach to designing learning objectives you may already know (as shown on the right in table 5-3).

Table 5-3. Marketing objectives dovetail with learning objectives.

Marketing Objective	Learning Objective
Audience (HR directors will . . .)	Audience (Participants will . . .)
Behavior (. . . sign up for a preview . . .)	Behavior (. . . name the four parts of a learning objective . . .)
Condition (. . . by faxing in a registration form . . .)	Condition (. . . using their notes . . .)
Date (. . . by the end of March.)	Degree (. . . with 100% accuracy.)

Here's another way to think about it: If marketing is about changing motivation to action, who do you want to do what by when? Just as with learning objectives, you want the behavior to be tangible—something that can be observed. Understanding the need for a class on business writing, for example, isn't enough. What do you want the learners to do about it? If your objective isn't linked to a tangible thing people can do, it won't be effective or measurable. Also, you need to be considerate in your choice of words. Getting people to register for a program doesn't mean they will attend, for example. Those are, in fact, two different objectives (though they might both be part of the same overall campaign).

4. Choose a Marketing Strategy

How many ways can you think of to market your products and services? Imagine you've just designed a stellar workplace safety program. Your objective is to get workers in a manufacturing plant (audience) to attend a pilot session you are offering (behavior) in your home office conference room (or—if you're internal—in your conference room) (condition) in one month (date). Can you name 10 marketing techniques you might use to achieve this objective? Jot them down on a piece of paper.

If you want to keep your training design interesting, you have to think past your first idea, past your tried and true techniques. You have to think quantity before quality. The same is true of marketing. That's why you were asked to think of 10 ideas, and not just three or four. The first few you wrote down are probably the ones you use all the time. Toward the bottom of your list are ideas that you probably haven't yet utilized or that you don't utilize often.

Take a look at table 5-4. How many of the marketing ideas presented here did you come up with in your brainstorm of marketing techniques?

In section 3, you'll find samples of several of these strategies. These can be used to start your own clipping file. It is very helpful to collect examples of marketing material that you respond to positively. They can be used to get ideas and to spark your creativity.

Your choice of a marketing strategy depends on your target audience and objectives, as well as a variety of other factors. For example, if your objective is to get new moms to test drive a minivan, you wouldn't put an ad in a car magazine or offer a discount for buying one. You would put it in a parent's magazine with a coupon for free baby clothes just for trying. Some print ads are more effective when the audience's buying motivations are based on fact (those with text and statistics). Other

Table 5-4. Fifty ways to market your training offerings.

Integrated

1. On performance reviews
2. In career development plans
3. As part of succession planning initiatives
4. Through individual learning plans
5. During a cross-training intervention
6. During new employee orientation
7. In paychecks
8. During needs assessments
9. On stationery
10. On business cards

Computer

11. Via email
12. Via intranet
13. Via Internet
14. CD-ROM

Telephone

15. On group voicemail messages
16. By individual solicitation

Face-to-Face

17. In current programs
18. At staff meetings
19. At organization-wide fairs
20. Through secret shoppers
21. Through a preview or demonstration
22. At an information booth
23. At committee meetings
24. At board meetings
25. At staff meetings
26. At a clinic
27. With actors serving as irate customers or disgruntled employees during a staff meeting, in a lunchroom, waiting in the reception area, or in some other "guerilla theater" performances
28. Via contests or raffle
29. Through word of mouth
30. Through referral awards

Media

31. Television
32. Radio
33. Videotape
34. Audiotape

Collateral (printed, written material)

35. Brochures
36. Books
37. Company newsletters
38. Direct mail
39. Catalogs
40. Name tents
41. Local newspapers
42. Training function newsletter
43. Trade publications
44. Postcards

Advertising

45. Table tents in public areas
46. Fliers in cars in lots and public areas
47. Signs or billboards
48. Banners and flags
49. Ticker tape display
50. Gifts and giveaways (mugs, mouse pads, pens, books, balloons, food)

ads are more effective when motivations are based on emotion (those with color and images). Pick more than one way to reach people—a blended approach.

Several other factors that help determine your choice of marketing strategies depend on whether you are marketing internally or externally, as shown in table 5-5.

Table 5-5. Factors that affect your choice of marketing strategy.

Marketing internally	vs.	Marketing from the "outside" (externally)
Development as a general concept	vs.	Development as a specific initiative
A single event	vs.	A series of events
A new product or service	vs.	An existing one

Your choice of marketing strategies will most likely change on different days. Even if you have to promote a specific CBT package this morning, you will have to promote development in your organization later in the afternoon. Even if you are promoting an internal event today, you may be asked to "sell" it to another organization in the future. Even if you are selling a new product today, you may revert to an old product tomorrow. Because you have many marketing needs and because one marketing strategy won't have universal appeal to your target audience, you don't just need one marketing strategy. You need several!

Let's look more closely at the factors that influence your choice of marketing strategies. Read on.

ARE YOU INTERNAL OR EXTERNAL? In addition to having different focuses for their marketing efforts, the techniques and resources at the disposal of internals and externals differ, as do their objectives. For example, an external may be able to suggest using group voicemail but usually does not have the ability to do so on his or her own. But externals, who are more motivated to market certain services because selling these services is actually what keeps them in business, might also be willing to spend on more costly marketing strategies.

DEVELOPMENT AS A GENERAL CONCEPT OR A SPECIFIC INITIATIVE. Promoting development as a concept is a steady, low-key process. You can't use gimmicks like hiring actors to stage a mock customer complaint as part of a guerilla theater strategy to promote development in an organization as you could to publicize a single event. Techniques for promoting development as a whole are more systematic.

ONE EVENT VERSUS A SERIES OF EVENTS. Trying to sell tickets to a baseball game between two infamous rival teams—say, the New York Yankees and the Boston Red Sox—is different from trying to sell season tickets to all of the Red Sox games. The goals of marketing these two events will differ, as will the approach. The same is true when you are trying to market one instance of training versus a whole catalog's worth of training. A single event could rely on such techniques as banners, parking lot fliers, announcements at staff meetings, and the like that wouldn't be as good a fit for marketing a series.

On the other hand, having a series of events to market at once can cut costs and opens up a wealth of new ways to present the information—training fairs, booklets, and brochures, to name a few. These are approaches that you cannot always easily justify for a single program.

NEW VERSUS EXISTING. The differences in marketing new and existing initiatives are subtle. There can be a lot of buzz and excitement about a new initiative. There can also be more doubt or skepticism. An existing program has a track record. Your marketing can include results achieved and customer testimonials. However, it is hard to maintain energy around existing programs. The marketing strategies you might use to launch an offering will differ from those you use to publicize one that's been offered monthly for the past year.

IMPRESSIONS. *Impressions* is the marketer's term for the total number of opportunities to come in contact with your message. This number is calculated by multiplying reach (the number of people your marketing might be seen by) by frequency (the number of times you expose this audience to your message). To illustrate, let's say you wanted to advertise your services on television. You decide to run the ad four times during "The Late Show" (most likely, you'll never do this, as this ad time costs

---

Myth: One factor that influences your choice of marketing strategy to use is whether the format of the training will be classroom or non-classroom.

Fact: Recent research by ASTD and the MASIE Center on what makes e-learning initiatives successful has shown that even for newer learning technologies, the marketing strategies that work are traditional. The preferred methods of course awareness for e-learning initiatives were emails and face-to-face. When the learning methodology is new and you anticipate people will be apprehensive about using it, traditional marketing helps make them more comfortable and assures them that things won't be so different.

upwards of $1 million per airing). If you know that 1 million people watch "The Late Show" and you are airing your ad four times, your number of impressions is 4 million.

Why learn this complex and technical term? This concept introduces you to the notion that you must be aware when selecting marketing strategies to consider all three things—how many people might you reach, how many times are you going to put the message out, and what is your potential impact when you multiply the two?

According to William Luther (2001), your frequency should be between five and 10 exposures. Much more than that and people start to weed out or even be turned off by your message. Much less than that and users will not get your message into their brains. You want to spread your communications out over time. You can't market too early and maintain momentum or enthusiasm. However, marketing early does help establish name recognition and help get the word out. If you don't start early enough, you won't fit in the recommended frequency.

AVAILABLE RESOURCES. Clearly, different marketing techniques require different levels of resources. Some, like promotional giveaways or glossy brochures with photographs, cost more than others, like mass email. Others, such as CD-ROMS or career development programs, take longer to execute than something like an announcement at a staff meeting. Some take only one person to complete, others a team of people.

And, one strategy isn't necessarily better than any other. In fact, if you opt for something expensive but don't properly utilize it, you're just wasting your money. The quality of the product is more important than how much time or money you spend.

The Final Marketing Tasks

The final three tasks in a marketing campaign—test, measure, and adapt—are covered in the next chapter. A form that summarizes all seven of the steps in this marketing campaign can be found in appendix B. You can use it as a template for planning the marketing aspects of your next training project.

* * *

What if you just don't have time for a high-quality marketing campaign in addition to everything else that you have to do? What are your options for support from others? Some people will have one or two additional options to turn to: working with an internal marketing or communications department; or working with an outside provider of marketing, public relations, or design services.

Denise Primrose has worked with two national nonprofit organizations as a development associate. In both positions, she had to promote her organization and its fundraising events. In her former position, she worked in a local office and received her marketing materials from an internal national design office. In her current position at National Brain Tumor Foundation, she does most of the marketing herself but hires external firms for larger projects. In table 5-6 she reviews some of the pros and cons with each of three working arrangements.

Why should you work with an internal communications or marketing department? An internal marketing or communications department can be a luxury for individuals who need to promote their products and services but are unable to do it themselves for any reason. The internal department is staffed with individuals whose expertise is promotion. Individuals do this type of work consistently and know the steps in the process and how they play out in your organization. They can provide a fresh set of eyes for your projects without needing time to get up to speed on organizational issues.

Table 5-6. Comparing three different ways to get your marketing done.

	Doing It Yourself	**Internal Marketing Department**	**External Marketing Firms**
Pros	• You can create a more personalized message.	• Using an internal department saves time. • Internal staff know the specific pieces you need and in what sequence (e.g., save-the-date card, brochure with registration, reminder). • That's their expertise; they've thought it out; the pieces are already in place. • They can come up with ideas you wouldn't have thought of.	• They can represent your organization in a professional manner to the public. • Larger marketing pieces are too burdensome to do internally. • They can come up with ideas you wouldn't have thought of.
Cons	• Marketing takes you away from other duties, logistics, and project management functions you need to do.	• You may have to compete with other departments for the attention of the internal marketing department.	• Their services are costly. • They do it because they're artists and they think differently than business people do (which is a con when conflicts of style arise, but can also be a pro).

An internal marketing department can benefit you by

- coordinating your look with the look of the organization as a whole
- providing company stock photo and video footage and organizational logos
- getting legal clearances and senior level endorsement
- using tools that you don't have (QuarkXPress, Microsoft Publisher, and the like) to create professional-quality materials for your programs
- working on sensitive, confidential, or competitive promotions for you that you could not send out to an external organization
- keeping the intellectual property inside the organization
- working faster than you probably can in their field of expertise.

An external organization that can assist in marketing provides many of the same benefits that an internal department can (table 5-7). Such companies are staffed by people whose expertise is in this type of work and they can provide a fresh set of eyes. They are also the only option for internal training and development professionals who need or desire help with their communications and do not have internal resources to provide it.

An external marketing department can benefit you by

- giving you an outsider's perspective
- providing expertise not existing in your organization
- telling you what other organizations are doing
- negotiating related discounts for printing, paper, mailing, and so on
- helping you strengthen industry and community links
- utilizing their relationships with the media in your community
- offering a broad range of specialized expert services in a cost-effective manner as they are provided on an as-needed basis
- helping you approach marketing in a more systematic way by uncovering what has worked, what hasn't, and why, or creating a yearly marketing plan.

Finding an external organization you can work with can be challenging. There are many of them out there that do similar work, and whether you like them depends on how well they do what they do and how you hit it off with them. Look for a good partner the same way that you would look for a good lawyer or doctor: Ask for referrals from friends or check professional associations, for a start. Do a little research at the library or on the Internet.

Once you find a potential service provider, you can ask a number of questions to find out if you will be a good match. Table 5-8 lists some important questions to ask and the types of responses you are looking for.

Table 5-7. What kind of external marketing organization should you work with?

Type of Organization	What the Organization Can Do for You
Graphic Design Firm	Takes your messages or materials and transforms them into informative, persuasive visual communications through a combination of type, color, and imagery.
Advertising Agency	Creates advertisements to be printed, read on the radio, or aired on TV, and coordinates the chosen media outlets to deliver the message.
Publicist	Promotes a discrete story or announcement to a specific audience using a variety of methods.
Press Agent	Provides information to the press, responds to media inquiries, and makes qualified experts available for comments or interviews.
Public Relations (PR) Firm	Creates, shapes, enhances, or changes public attitudes and perceptions. PR firms employ both publicists and press agents and provide a comprehensive set of services to promote the interests and images of their clients.
Marketing Firm	Assists you with product development, pricing, promotion, and distribution strategies. Some firms conduct research about what products customers want and appropriate pricing. Other firms assume specific promotion and sales responsibilities for their clients.

So now that you've found the perfect match in a provider of marketing, communications, or PR services, it's time to turn the tables. To be a good client of one of these service providers, you should

- be as specific as you can when asking for quotes; that way there will be no surprises later on and it will be possible for you to compare service providers.
- only commit to one project at a time.
- put deadlines in writing.
- don't select based solely on price. Balance costs with talent and knowledge.
- specify who will be responsible for each phase and task of the program.
- be clear about goals, objectives, timeline, and budget.

Table 5-8. Finding a good match in an external communications or PR organization.

Ask These Questions . . .	. . . and Look for Responses That . . .
Who are you?	Fit with your style, approach.
Can I see a sample of your best work?	Reflect the services and products you are considering purchasing. Don't pay attention to fancy graphics, for example, if you are looking for a writer. Try to see real-life samples, as opposed to samples displayed in a portfolio or book. And ask for results of the campaigns you review.
Who are your current and past clients?	Indicate the company has worked with reputable organizations similar to yours. Ask for a list of references you can contact to create a profile on your potential partner.
How long have they been, or how long were they your clients?	Reflect repeat, long-term customers.
What is your specific experience in our industry?	Describe previous jobs or projects similar to the one for which you might contract for services.
Who would work on our account and what are their credentials?	Ensure that the organization doesn't pass all the work off to unsupervised interns.
What has been your organization's turnover rate in personnel over the past five years?	Seem to show low turnover so that you know that the work in their portfolio was done by the people who will be doing your work.
How are your fees determined? What do your prices include?	Include reasonable revisions without new charges unless you add new information. What bulk discounts can the organization pass along to you? Would the staff be willing to do any services at low cost in exchange for promoting their company in your materials?
What is your normal learning curve or ramp-up period, and when might we begin to see the results of your efforts on our behalf?	Suggest a short ramp-up period. You, as the client, will set the timeline for deliverables. Results should be apparent from the first deadline.

- know how much can you pay. What is your real budget? Look at what you have budgeted for marketing over time versus what was actually spent.
- provide what in the training and development field is called a request for proposals (RFP), but in marketer's terms is known as a "backgrounder" for your company.

This final item—the backgrounder—should include your organization's history (size, products, services, date founded, and so forth) and mission, marketing needs as they are presently perceived, marketing expectations, any special skills or resources being sought, a summary of current or past marketing efforts, requirements for overall "look and feel" (for example, company logo on all deliverables), budget parameters, initial length of contact with selected firm, and special circumstances that may affect any aspect of the program.

Gearing Up for Your Campaign

Whether you are working on your own marketing campaign, or whether you've enlisted the help of others, there are several considerations to be made when deciding how to inform your target audience of your products or services that will meet their needs. The next time you are writing a project plan, take some time to make these considerations and incorporate marketing tasks into your rollout plan. You may see significant improvements in getting informed, targeted audience members to turn their motivation into action. The next chapter will tell you how to gauge the improvements you might make.

Now What?

With what ideas or actionable ideas should you walk away from this chapter?

- Incorporate the seven marketing tasks into your usual project plans:
    - Define target audience.
    - Identify audience preferences and motivators.
    - Establish *ABCD* marketing objectives.
    - Choose a marketing solution.
    - Test.
    - Measure.
    - Adapt.

- All these factors influence how you market your training—internal or external, concept or initiative, one or a series, new or existing, frequency, impressions, fit for your target audience, and available resources.

- Use the marketing plan in appendix B to remember all steps.

Chapter Six

Building on Your Success

✳✳✳

 ## A **Quick** Look

Measuring the effects of marketing is always a challenge, but it is even more so for marketers of training products, which often are not tangible products, for example, cell phones, so you can't just count how many are eventually sold. There are, however, several lessons that can be learned from other industries when it comes to measuring the effectiveness of marketing. For instance, you can learn to recognize which aspect of the campaign it's important to measure, understand that results will take time to measure, and know that you can use market tracking data to refine both your marketing and your products or services.

Chapter **Features**

* Seven lessons from other industries about tracking marketing effectiveness
* Nine simple techniques for tracking the effectiveness of marketing training and development
* Questions to consider when your campaign is successful—or not so successful
* Competencies addressed:
  — Maintenance/evaluation
  — Cost-benefit analysis
  — Project planning

Measuring the Effectiveness of Your Marketing

Imagine for a moment that you run the marketing function for a credit card company. You send out tens of millions of direct mail solicitations per year. How do you determine which of these solicitations are effective? What are the variables you can test to make that determination?

Population Test

One type of test you might do is a population test. For example, you could send the same marketing solicitation to different groups of people. Your credit card company can purchase lists of individuals, for example, who are members of a particular organization, who have recently moved, or who subscribe to a particular magazine. This way, you can track which groups of individuals are most likely to apply for one of your cards.

Offer Test

You can also test different types of products as part of an offer test. For example, you may try mailing individuals from the same market segment different types of credit cards—one with a high credit line and another with a low interest rate. You can also send different offer types to diverse populations—combining a population test with a population test—to measure the likelihood of people responding to your varied products and what type of person does.

You can also test which incentives are most popular. Will more people apply for a card if they receive a box of chocolates, or if they receive a T-shirt, just for applying?

Creative Test

You can do what's called a creative test, *creative* being the marketer's term for the look, feel, and message of the marketing materials. In this type of test, you send out the same offer, but you use versions of the marketing materials that vary in appearance or "sound." For example, one may have a photograph of a busy family and a customer testimonial emphasizing the convenience of the product, and another may feature a graph depicting how much money one could save by consolidating other credit card balances on this card. On the simplest level, a creative test can determine whether having a blue or red background is more effective.

Marketing Channel Test

You can test different marketing channels. Is it more effective to mail a solicitation or to put an application on the back of an airline ticket? Does it make sense to telephone a prospective customer or to advertise on his or her favorite Website?

Evaluating Your Test Results

Regardless of the test you use as the head of marketing for the credit card company, how will you determine whether you have been successful? First, there is the obvious measure—response rate. How many people responded to your offer by submitting an application? But, if your analysis of your marketing success ends there, you will likely be misled; the prospects most likely to respond are probably not your best customers. You'd also want to know how many of those who submitted applications were actually approved for a credit card. Did these customers pay their balances in full or make only the minimum payment? Were their payments on time or frequently late? This data obviously can take years to collect but, if collected and analyzed, it can serve as a powerful tool to identify the best marketing tactics as they relate to the bottom line.

Applying Marketing Lessons to Training

What can you, as a training and development professional, learn from the approach to testing marketing campaigns taken by this true-to-life credit card company? Many things, including these seven lessons:

1. It is difficult to evaluate the overall effectiveness of a campaign and easier to focus on a particular aspect of that campaign, be it the marketing materials themselves, the respondents, or the marketing techniques you used.
2. Marketing is a long-term activity. Results will take time to measure.
3. You need procedures and resources in place to record and analyze marketing data over time.
4. When thinking about whom you want to reach with your marketing, consider who makes an ideal candidate now and who will be a good candidate

over the long haul. For example, it would be wonderful to get six new clients for your consulting business, but you don't want to waste all your energy now on a client who won't prove profitable over the long term.

5. Use marketing data to refine not only your marketing strategies but your products and services, as well. For example, if you are having a poor response rate to a CBT program, you can first refine how you are marketing it. But, you might also try varying the product itself to see if that is what really needs to be improved. Or, if you find that personal calls are more effective than mass e-mails in your marketing efforts, use them. If you find out that more people sign up for a half-day workshop than a full-day one, see how many classes you can shorten.

6. In the test-measure-adapt model, the result is learning—learning which marketing approaches are effective and learning which groups respond to the marketing of your products and services. In this model, there really isn't a way to fail, only a way to improve.

7. It is difficult to track response rates. There is often a lapse between the time you send out the marketing piece and when people respond. During that time, they could have had three other exposures to your product or service. Now, to which marketing strategy can you attribute their response?

How Do I Apply Marketing Principles?

My organization, the TrainingSource, estimates that $1,700,000 is the extremely conservative target market for our organization over the next five years. How did we arrive at that number? We had to do some number crunching.

   First, we got labor market information from the California Employment Development Department. We learned the total number of employees in the county and the total number in the three industries we were targeting. That way, we were able to calculate the total number of employees in our target markets—195,000. ASTD's *State of the Industry Report 2001* states that, on average, organizations spend $700 per year per employee on training. If $700 is spent on training per employee, and our target audience is 195,000, then we are talking about a $136,500,000 market.

   We were able to compare how much we currently brought in to that figure to assess our own market share. To set a goal for what our market share should be, we factored in the percentage of training dollars that are outsourced on a national average (between 25% and 34%) and decided what percentage of that number we would feel comfortable with. It was far more than we were currently doing. Our new goal is to achieve a 5% market share of the total outsourced training dollars in our county; in equation form this is $136,500,000 \times 25\% \times 5\% = \$1,706,250$.

Susan Pedergnana, director of business development and marketing, The TrainingSource, an affiliate of the San Mateo County Community College District

When you cannot systematically track your marketing effectiveness because you don't have the procedures in place, because you can't figure out what people are responding to, or for any other reason, there are some simple (albeit less scientific) ways to get a gauge of how your marketing is doing. For example:

- Look back at your marketing objectives and see whether you didn't meet, met, or exceeded them.
- Add "How did you hear about this product/service/workshop" questions to all of your existing surveys, applications, and forms.
- Conduct an in-house audit. Simply count the number of mentions about the particular product or service that users might see. Make notes about their prominence in organizational materials. For example, are training events mentioned on the front page of the employee newsletter or just in the middle? How many column inches does training get in the newsletter?
- Track how many individuals have given you permission to provide them with more information or to contact them again. Count the number of qualified leads you have for your external products or services. Count the number of advocates you have for your internal training function.
- Both externals and internals must know their market shares. Internals can track the percentage of employees (unique individuals, not repeat customers) who have taken advantage of any training opportunities or the percentage of training that is going on organizationally that they are providing. Externals will want to know how much of the market they've saturated.
- Track the amount of training that is going on organization-wide, by department or work group, and by the number of employees going to outside training providers or conferences. Compare how much mandatory versus elective training is being completed.
- Assess the standing of the training and development function in the minds of your customers. Ask questions such as, "How is training perceived in your department?" or "How do you think the training function is regarded organizationally?" Have them evaluate your department using a four-point scale instead of a five-point scale on which they can pick the middle, noncommittal choice.
- Track your marketing costs per employee or per client. That is, divide the cost of your marketing by the number of people you are trying to reach or by the number of employees in your organization.
- Mimic professional marketing firms that hold focus groups or interview random individuals about their reactions to marketing campaigns.

Marketing is not your primary job, but applying some marketing testing techniques can help you in your primary job, can assist you in determining what type of marketing is effective and worthwhile, and will produce the results you hope to achieve. Marketing is not a standalone activity. It is an activity that promotes and informs the rest of your work and helps with business planning.

Are You Ready for Success?

What if you used all of your marketing testing data to plan a campaign that was utterly successful? What if you doubled the number of people who attended a conference you were hosting from one year to the next?

Great! But, are you prepared for achieving the results you hoped for? Sometimes it is hard to start thinking in the mindset of abundance when you usually have to pull teeth to get people to sign up for your programs. But, when you focus on marketing, and it starts to be successful, you have to be ready to raise and respond to these types of questions:

- Is your conference set up to accommodate twice as many people as the year before?
- Do you have a solid process in place for handling waiting lists?
- Do you have a system for setting priorities for registration and the waiting list? In other words, should a process other than first-come, first-served be utilized? Should someone who's already been on the wait list for the class have first priority the next time it is offered?
- Should individuals be limited in the number of workshops overall, or in a specific topic area, that they can sign up for? For some programs, it may become necessary to limit participation to those for whom there is a direct business need. You may have to give first priority to someone whose performance evaluation indicates that they need an intervention like yours in order to move from unsatisfactory to satisfactory.
- Should people pay for classes if they don't show up, especially if you are maintaining a waiting list and you didn't have time to call someone for that spot? How would these penalties be perceived organizationally? (See chapter 3 for more about no-show fees.)
- How are you going to let people know about your processes for standing room only, waiting list priority, and no-shows? (The manager's guide in appendix A introduces some of these concepts to Redwood City employees in the section called Frequently Asked Questions.)

- What about deciding to add another section of the conference, perhaps one that runs concurrently in a different location or one that takes place on another day?

  — If you add another section, should you just leave all the existing registrants in the original conference and assign new participants to the additional section?
  — What if the new section would actually be better for someone who's in the original section? Do you want to give him or her the option to switch?
  — If too many original participants want to move to the new section, what then?
  — Do you have the money to continue to add sections of a program, or will you have to go to other departments to ask them to pay for additional courses their employees want?
  — If you're using an external provider for the additional section, can you get a discount on the second section?

- What's your plan for handling walk-ins for your classroom programs?

  — When do you allow walk-ins to enter—before all your conference participants have arrived or after the program has started?
  — What if walk-ins have already gone inside and then a late-arriving registrant appears?
  — How will you handle prework for classes that draw walk-ins?
  — How should you follow up with potential walk-ins who aren't able to get in? Do you keep them on your list of prospects?

Issues such as registration priority, participant criteria, and increasing capacity pertain to e-learning and other forms of initiatives, too. Are you prepared to support lots of e-learners? Is there a limit? If you are only getting 25 licenses now, what is the incremental cost of adding more later on? You must consider all these questions when you set your marketing goals. In other words, if you build it and they do come, are you ready for them?

And, what if, despite your best marketing efforts, you don't meet your goals? What are the related issues in this instance and how do you handle them? Do you cancel the program? Think about these considerations:

- Is it a sequential program? Will canceling one mean you have people who can't attend the next?
- Has it not been offered in a while?

- When will it be offered next?
- What is the cost to cancel in terms of money, morale, and other factors?
- How many other recent programs have you canceled?
- Who is registered? Who isn't?
- Is it tied to an immediate business need?

Simply marketing your efforts and counting the number of responses you get provides an incomplete picture of how effective your marketing efforts are. Especially if you are spending a great deal on marketing, it is important to institute some units of measurement into your campaign. Additionally, you need to be prepared to respond to marketing that either does its job in spades or fails to do so.

Now What?

With what ideas or actionable ideas should you walk away from this chapter?

- Do you want to do a population test, an offer test, a test of popular incentives, a creative test, or a test of marketing channels?

- Response rate is not enough. The best audience members may not be those who respond immediately—repeat customers, for example.

- Results will take time to measure. Remember that marketing is a long-term activity.

- Use the data to refine your marketing strategies—and your products and services.

- In the test-measure-adapt model, the result is learning: learning which marketing would be more effective and learning what people respond to about your products and services. In this model, there really isn't a way to fail, only to improve.

- It is difficult to track response rate due to time lapses and other influences on the recipients.

- Know what percentage of the market you have.

- Marketing is not a standalone activity. It is an activity that promotes and informs the rest of your work and helps with business planning.

- You must be prepared to handle the challenges that come with successful marketing of your training and development programs.

Chapter Seven

How to Write Like a Marketer

****

 ## A **Quick Look**

Forget the eloquent narrative writing you learned in school, forget your proper grammar. Writing marketing copy (that's the marketer's term for the words) is a completely different practice. There are words and phrases and ways of presenting them that are particular to this kind of communication. Marketing writing takes into account research on personality types, types of readers, and words that are most likely to convert motivation into action. Marketing isn't all bells and whistles; it's crisp, compelling writing that anyone can learn.

Chapter **Features**

* Twenty-one tips for writing like a marketer
* Samples of good marketing copy
* Ideas for titling your initiatives
* Competencies addressed:
  — Written and verbal presentation
  — Creativity

Techniques for Writing Marketing Copy

Any of these sound familiar?

- You may have already won!
- Act now. Supplies are limited.
- Don't be the only one on your block without it!
- Be the first one on your block to own it.
- Has this ever happened to you?
- Inside: 101 tips for landing a spouse.
- How to get thin thighs in 30 days.

When people think about how marketers write, some of the first impressions that come to mind are lines like the ones you just read. Although these may seem overused, trite, or inapplicable to marketing of training, there is much to be learned from the marketing techniques they build upon.

Why is it, for example, that you can put out an email announcing an upcoming Excel workshop one week and not get any takers, but put out the same email a week later, with only the addition of the words "three seats left," and end up with a waiting list? This "limited time" marketing technique relies on words like "space is limited," "limited time offer," and "limited release." It spurs people into action. Those who were planning to register and just hadn't gotten around to it feel that they'd better do it or lose their chance. People who were on the fence now believe that this is going to be a popular class, one that others think is worthwhile. And there are other tried and true techniques.

"Don't be the only one on your block without it" is an example of the bandwagon technique. This technique capitalizes on people's desire to be included. This technique brought about campaigns that state "50 successful CEOs have completed this program" or "People just like you have benefited from attending this workshop in the following ways . . . ."

An extension of the bandwagon approach is the inclusion of testimonials—actual comments from past users of the products or services. For example, to help create positive buzz about a mandatory new employee orientation program, you can include quotations from past participants on the invitation (figure 7-1).

Testimonials should be as specific as possible. "It was good" is not going to be as effective as something like, "The activities made me aware of how decisions are made in each department . . . ." A good testimonial stresses results, as in ". . . With that knowledge, I was able, when I needed a decision from another department, to provide the information necessary for them to make that decision quickly and with little additional input from me." Use natural-sounding testimonials that do not sound too polished. When a testimonial can help allay a potential de-motivator, it is especially useful, like "I didn't think this online program was going to address my specific concerns, but the real-time help feature allowed me to communicate with a live person who helped me sort out my issue."

Getting a testimonial that you can use isn't always easy. Sometimes, you'll over-hear what could be a perfect testimonial and need to get it written down on paper. Sometimes what is written on a program evaluation or other documentation isn't clear or complete. You'll have to be willing to ask, "Can I write down what you just told me?" or "Do you mind if write down what I just overheard and use it for marketing?" or "Thank you for your favorable evaluation. Would it be alright if I edited it and used it for marketing purposes?" Just be sure that you procure per-mission from the person providing the comment, transcribe the comment accu-rately, and give proper attribution if appropriate.

Here's an example of how you can apply these techniques to marketing of your training and development programs. Here is how this line: "E-learning is coming to ABC Company! Sign up now for a free preview" would sound utilizing each of the techniques:

- *Limited time technique:* The first six people to sign up for the e-learning preview will receive a Blackberry wireless communicator.
- *Bandwagon:* In 1999, ASTD reported that 39.8 percent of U.S. organiza-tions in its benchmarking survey were using e-learning for training. It is among the fastest growing learning technologies for learning anytime, anywhere. Now, it's coming to ABC Company! Come find out what 39.8 percent already know.
- *Testimonial:* "I acquired some great skills that will be useful to me as I advance to a management position at ABC Company through e-learning and I did it on my own time." Come find out how you can, too, at our preview.

Figure 7-1. Including testimonials in an invitation to a training event.

As a new employee, you are scheduled to attend our next entertaining and engaging
New Employee Welcome (NEW)!

Welcome to the City of Redwood City

What NEW includes:

- A breakfast reception with Department Heads
- A tour of the City
- A condensed version of our Relentless Customer Service program
- Lunch with the City Manager
- Games, videos, and more!

No dull lectures here!

Some goals of NEW:

- Welcome you to the City
- Introduce you to some of the City's key players and to your colleagues in other departments
- Provide you some basic information about how the City operates and resources available to you
- Review some general Citywide policies, including safety and harassment
- Help you discover how to bring our City values to life

The reviews are in!

- "The program was well planned with fun activities! A lot better than expected!"
- "Helped psych me up for my job!"
- "Great program! Informative, enjoyable, and a great way to meet other new employees from various departments."
- "Fun! Fun! Fun!"

Logistics:

Thursday, June 6, 2002, 8:30 a.m. to 3:30 p.m.—
   Meet in City Hall Council Chambers
Friday, June 7, 2002, 8:30 a.m. to 12:00 p.m.—
   Meet in City Hall lobby for a bus tour
All meals will be provided

RSVP:

All newly hired employees are expected to complete this program in their first few months of employment. It is a lot of time to be away from your new job, but it is not time wasted! And, it'll never get easier to get away, so don't put it off "until next time."

Please RSVP to Sophie Oberstein at extension 5956 by June 3 so she can get an accurate headcount.

Now, it's your turn to try these writing techniques. Take a look at figure 7-2, which consists of an activity to start you thinking in the mindset of a marketing copy writer.

Tips to Write Like a Marketing Pro

The idea is not simply to plug whatever copy you have into one of these techniques. First of all, when used improperly, they can seem insincere and awkward. Marketing materials are often slick- looking, state-of-the-art, glossy, and graphic-intensive material, but, when you wipe away the graphics and formatting, there must be substance underneath. The words you use to describe your product or program must be compelling, engaging, and well thought out. Second, above all, you must be truthful in your marketing. That's the first of 21 tips for writing like a marketer:

1. Be truthful.
2. Know your audience.
3. Be culturally relevant.
4. Variety is key.

Figure 7-2. Now you try it: writing marketing copy.

Activity

Take the following line, or one for an upcoming product or program of your own, and rewrite it using the previously described techniques. Then, you can look at the suggestions that appear after the activity.

> Stress is all around us. Work is stressful. Finding time for a life outside of work is stressful. And, outside life can be stressful, too. We are a consulting firm that specializes in stress management assessments and seminars. Let us show your company what we can do for you!

- *Limited time:*

- *Bandwagon:*

- *Testimonial:*

Did your ideas look anything like these?

- *Limited time:* We'll provide 100 free stress assessments at your company in the month of March if you sign up by February 15.
- *Bandwagon:* We have provided stress reduction seminars at more than 100 companies in your regional area and we want to show you what we can do for you!
- *Testimonial:* "After one of this company's seminars, I was able to prioritize my working hours and to incorporate quick relaxation breaks throughout my day that make me feel relaxed and ready to work!"

---

5. If there is star power, use it.
6. Make it seem selective.
7. Make marketing positive.
8. Highlight your unique selling proposition.
9. Have fun, break the mold.
10. Require a response.
11. Stress benefits, not features.
12. Support with statistics and research studies.
13. Have themes.
14. Educate while you market.
15. Have something new to offer or announce.
16. Pique their interest.
17. Write simply.
18. Use the active voice.
19. Make sure you copyedit.
20. Use tentative language.
21. Pilot your copy.

A Closer Look at Tips to Write Like a Marketing Pro

So, how can you use the above tips to enhance your marketing writing? Read on.

1. BE TRUTHFUL. Not only is it ethical to be truthful in marketing, if you aren't, your marketing is sure to backfire. The next time you try to reach potential learners, they won't believe you. Don't be like the boy who cried, "Wolf!" Don't exaggerate the benefits of a program. Don't promote learning outcomes that will not be possible. To summarize in terms you may be personally familiar with, don't tell them "You may have already won."

2. KNOW YOUR AUDIENCE. You want to know how the members of your target audience are likely to react to your writing and to the message that writing is conveying. Are they avid readers, skimmers, or scanners? What style of reading matter do they prefer—academic, technical, satirical, or informal? Do they appreciate creative or cute writing, or does it turn them off? Is English their first language? What is their reading level?

Have they read many similar messages from other sources in the recent past? How can your message be misinterpreted? Are there any issues that are going to cloud how your message is received? For example, if you think they might see your material and think, "Oh, just another flavor of the month," don't ignore it—use it!

"Think this is just the newest flavor of the month? Think again. ABC Company needs to change the way we provide customer service. We haven't introduced a new model in more than two years, and we've made investments in this process that we know will be long-term and far-reaching."

3. BE CULTURALLY RELEVANT. Use language that is global and inclusive. For example, use gender-neutral pronouns when possible (*you, one, they*) or alternate "he" and "she" in alternating sections or examples. Be aware of how other cultures, nations, or religions might read your copy. Avoid idioms, metaphors, and slang that may not translate well. Know, for example, that when you use the word *American,* people in other countries don't know if you mean North America, South America, or Canada. Words like *overseas* and *foreign* are ethnocentric; they put the United States at the center of the universe. ("Countries outside the United States" is better.)

4. VARIETY IS KEY. Especially for a training function that communicates on an ongoing basis with its target audience, if all of your communications sound the same, they'll get tuned out. Figure 7-3 presents a series of email messages sent out over the course of one month to communicate upcoming training events. The emails were entirely textual so that readers did not have to take an extra step to open an attachment and so that even those with slower older machines could open them with ease.

5. IF THERE IS STAR POWER, USE IT. Even if you write the marketing copy, see if you can get it to come from senior management or top authority. If senior-level folks are involved in any aspect of the product or service you are describing, mention it.

6. MAKE IT SEEM SELECTIVE. Use the "limited seats available" approach. But, only use it if seats *are* limited. If you say that there's a waiting list for a classroom program but then there are several empty seats, you'll be found out and lose your credibility. Make people apply to participate in certain pilot programs or new initiatives. Give senior-level management the criteria by which to nominate employees for certain initiatives.

7. MAKE MARKETING POSITIVE. There is a fine line between making people aware of their blind spots and making them feel insulted. For example, consider this statement: "Last year, U.S. companies employing 500 or more employees spent an average of $30 million on worker's compensation claims. Come find out how you can help ABC Company avoid these costly claims." Compare that to this statement,

**Figure 7-3. A series of emails for marketing
training and development classes and activities.**

DATE: February 20, 2002
SUBJECT: Coming in March

Read on to learn more about upcoming employee training and development opportunities:
- Word, Level I. Friday, March 8. A good overview course for beginning computer users. Topics include Word basics, navigating, formatting, tabs and tables, page appearance, tools, and printing. 8:30 a.m.–4 p.m., Library Small Meeting Room.
- Listening. Wednesday, March 13. Reflecting is a critical active listening skill and learning (or relearning) to use it is the only objective of this two-hour workshop on enhancing your communication skills. This course is a prerequisite for the conflict resolution workshop coming up in July. 9–11 a.m. or 1–3 p.m., City Hall Room 1C.
- City Talk Toastmasters. Wednesdays. A Toastmasters Club has been formed for Redwood City employees and members of the community. The Toastmasters Club provides a structured skill development process for enhancing your public speaking and presentation skills. Drop in to see what it's all about. Or, if you have a presentation you need to practice in front of a group, call extension 5956 to get an upcoming agenda. Wednesdays, 12:30–1:30 p.m., City Hall.

DATE: March 2, 2002
SUBJECT: It Takes Two

Two lunchtime walks are scheduled for those who want to get in shape with us—Tuesday, April 30 from City Hall and Thursday, May 2 from the CAB. Both walks are from 12:30–1:00 p.m.

Two hours is all it takes to get recharged about customer service. A two-hour workshop is being held Friday, May 3, from 10:30 a.m.–12:30 p.m. in City Hall.

Only two weeks left until the start of the next conversational Spanish class. Please, register by 2 p.m. on 2sday (Tuesday!). The class is six weeks long and will be held on Thursdays from 1–2 p.m. in the main library.

Finally, we are offering two additional sections of the listening workshop on May 14. This workshop is a prerequisite for the conflict resolution program scheduled for July 24, 2002.

DATE: March 14, 2002
SUBJECT: Countdown

Six weeks left in the intermediate Spanish class. Seats available.
Five weeks until the next NEW on April 11 and 12. Invitations to new hires are in the mail!
Four days until the next meeting of the newsletter committee. Lunch is included! (March 18, 12–1)
Three seats left in the Microsoft Windows class on May 20. This is a perfect introduction to computing!
Two is the level of Excel instruction being offered on Tuesday, March 26.
One brown bag discussion is being held on March 15 (tomorrow). We'll provide popcorn and a movie and a chance to interact with your colleagues in other departments.

(continued on next page)

**Figure 7-3. A series of emails for marketing
training and development classes and activities (continued).**

DATE: March 17, 2002
SUBJECT: Handling Difficult Customers

Have you heard the story about Wade Boggs, former third baseman for the Boston Red Sox? It seems that whenever his team played in New York at Yankee Stadium, there was one heckler in the box seats close to the field who would shout obscenities and insults. "Boggs, you stink!" he'd yell.

Do you have customers like that? Don't you sometimes wish you had the right comeback? Don't you wish you could improve the situation? Boggs's response did just that. To find out how Boggs handled the unruly fan, and other strategies for dealing with difficult customers, sign up for the March 28 workshop.*

DATE: March 18, 2002
SUBJECT: Puede leer esto?

Si quiere practicar su español o aprender algo nuevo en un ambiente seguro con otros empleados de ABC, con una profesora fabulosa, venga a la clase Basic Spanish Conversation.

DATE: March 19, 2002
SUBJECT: Fear of public speaking?

Fear of speaking in public is second only to fear of death for many adults. Does your heart race at just the thought of speaking in front of a group? Whether the group you need to address is big (hundreds of people) or small (your supervisor), whether the group is for social or business purposes, the skills that Toastmasters can provide are invaluable.

To find out more about this group that has helped more than 5 million people worldwide improve their presentation and leadership skills since 1924, please plan to attend a meeting. Wednesdays, 12:30–1:30 p.m., City Hall.

DATE: March 24, 2002
SUBJECT: How might you respond?

What would you say if someone told you, "My department gets short shrift around here! I feel like people only pay attention to what happens in the bigger departments, and we don't get any attention. Maybe I should transfer to R&D, then I'd get noticed!"?

A. I know what you mean. R&D gets more attention than my department does, too!
B. You feel like people in the larger departments get better recognition.
C. Maybe you should talk to your boss about that. That seems like a really important issue!
D. Wow! It's terrible to work in one of the smaller departments!

If your answer was A, C, or D, you might want to add a new listening tool to your tool belt—reflecting. Reflecting is a critical active listening skill. And, listening is a critical skill for customer service and conflict resolution.

We are holding two workshop sessions on the skill of reflective listening on May 14. (By the way, if you want to know why B was the best answer, look at the bottom of this message.) In this interactive, skill-based workshop, you'll learn (or review) the skills of reflective listening. This course is a prerequisite for the July 24 conflict resolution workshop. It is also one way for employees hired after January 1, 2002, to fulfill their new hire pathway requirements. To register, sign onto LEAP. May 14, 1–3 p.m. or 5–7 p.m., conference room 2B.
Instructor:

> So, what about responses A, B, C, or D?
> A. I know what you mean. R&D gets more attention than my department does, too! Responses like this one begin to turn the spotlight away from the speaker and onto the person who is supposed to be doing the listening.
> B. You feel like people in the larger departments get better recognition. This is the best choice in this scenario because it remains focused on the speaker, and it attempts to reflect back the essence of what the speaker is trying to say.
> C. Maybe you should talk to your supervisor about that. That seems like a really important issue! Our natural inclination (and it's not a bad one) is to give advice or to try to help solve the problem. The problem with jumping into solutions too fast is that the speaker doesn't always have a chance to fully express his or her feelings or to actually define what the real problem is.
> D. Wow! It's terrible to work in one of the smaller departments! Empathy is nice, but it's not the same as listening. Also, it often puts a label on the situation that might not be entirely what the speaker had in mind.

* One day, Boggs decided he had had enough. He walked directly over to the fan and asked, "Are you the guy who's always yelling at me?" "Yeah, it's me," his tormentor replied. "What are you going to do about it?" Boggs took a new baseball out of his pocket, autographed it, tossed it to the man, and went back to the field. The man supposedly never yelled at Boggs again, illustrating Abraham Lincoln's saying, "I destroy my enemy when I make him my friend."

which is more likely to make people feel like they are being spoken down to: "Your department has experienced a level of worker's compensation claims consistently higher than the national average. Come to a seminar on how to reduce these claims." This kind of marketing establishes training as a punishment.

8. HIGHLIGHT YOUR UNIQUE SELLING PROPOSITION. Make sure your marketing points out what is different and better about your products or services than your competitors'. Even if you are internal and don't really think you have competitors, you have to realize that there are plenty of companies out there that do exactly what you do. You can do it better because you are internal and you are more familiar with the organization's culture and the needs of your audience. What's your niche? What is exclusively yours? What is outstanding that differentiates your services? What's different about this class from any other one your target audience may have taken previously?

9. HAVE FUN, BREAK THE MOLD. Let your copy sound different from the rest. But remember to consider the tastes of your audience. Also realize that humor is easy to misunderstand. Sarcasm, for example, can be detected when people are hearing the words but not as often when they are reading the words.

Titles offer an opportunity to inject some fun into your copywriting. Titles for workshops or materials are important in setting the tone, describing the content, and helping to sell your offerings. Headlines should be nine words or less.

Research by David Ogilvy (1985) shows that five times more people read headlines and titles than they do the body copy that accompanies them. In addition, Ogilvy concludes that titles or headlines that promise benefits are read four times more often than those that don't promise any. *Communication Briefings,* a periodical for newsletter editors, suggests these as effective types of titles:

- *Familiar sayings with a twist:* Easy as A-B-See (optometrist).
- *Use of opposites:* Saving big is no small task.
- *Inclusion of statistics and facts:* More Generation Xers believe in UFOs than believe Social Security will be around when they retire.
- *Testimonial and endorsement:* Michael Jordan says fly United.
- *How-to statements:* How to win the lottery.
- *Use of unusual or large numbers:* 2 and 1/2 reasons why mentoring is important; 450 ways to coach employees; learn four ways to recognize employees.

Similarly, you can have fun and set yourself (or your organization) apart by the title you choose for yourself. Nance Cheifetz is the corporate fairy godmother; salespeople at Charthouse Learning are called idea generators; Nancy Miller is a clutterologist; and David Parks of tompeterscompany! is creator of ClientWOW!

10. REQUIRE A RESPONSE. You have an objective for each piece of marketing. To achieve that objective, you have to ask for some action on the part of your readers. Fax in this form, call this number, attend this meeting, or answer this question. Make sure readers know what to do with the material you've provided them. Even if you think they know what you want them to do, spell it out. Otherwise, you've not closed the sale.

11. STRESS BENEFITS, NOT FEATURES. Features are the same for everyone who will participate. For example, "You'll receive a copy of the facilitator's latest book. It has great graphics and a helpful glossary." Features won't necessarily sell a product or service. Benefits are descriptions of why these features might appeal to us or help us. Where features are universal, benefits are customized. So, for the person who doesn't like to read dense text, the graphics in the book will enable him or her to get the main points visually, without having to read a lengthy explanation. For those who skim text, a glossary can ensure that they are familiar with important terms. For a little practice putting this writing tip to work, try the activity in figure 7-4.

Figure 7-4. Now you try it: changing features to benefits.

Change these features to benefits. The first example is done for you.

- Feature: Easy-to-use indexed reference guide is included.
- Benefit: When you forget what you learned, you can locate the topic on an extensive index and be reminded.

- Feature: This workshop is offered via the intranet.
- Benefit:

- Feature: This workshop provides definitions of features and benefits.
- Benefit:

Did your statements look anything like these?
- You can have your employees complete this workshop at their desks when work is slow, which will increase overall productivity.
- You need to know what a benefit is if you want creative marketing copy that is compelling.

---

12. SUPPORT WITH STATISTICS AND RESEARCH STUDIES. Research in *Communications Briefings* shows that use of statistics is the most effective type of "proof" in marketing. On the other hand, 70.8 percent of statistics are made up on the spot, so make sure yours are thoroughly reputable and documented. (By the way, that 70.8 statistic was one of those made-up ones.)

13. HAVE THEMES. Themes help people to chunk information, which in turn aids familiarity, memory, and responsiveness. Themes are useful for organizing content and serving as a consistent element in a marketing campaign.

14. EDUCATE WHILE YOU MARKET. Your overall objective is to develop employees, so do so even in your marketing. Recognize the opportunity that marketing affords you to reach a broader audience than your actual intervention will reach, so use it as a teachable moment.

15. HAVE SOMETHING NEW TO OFFER OR ANNOUNCE. Notices or communications without a real purpose can cross the line to junk mail or its electronic counterpart, spam. Make sure every piece of material you distribute has a purpose.

16. PIQUE THEIR INTEREST. Don't give everything away in your marketing. Leave them wanting more, like a good movie trailer does.

17. WRITE SIMPLY. Present content in a crisp, simple, compelling manner. Clarity, organization, and simplicity help the reader quickly and easily understand your message. Multisyllabic words (like multisyllabic) should be avoided wherever possible. Don't write: "Utilize a multi-tined instrument to ingest starchy carbohydrates," when you mean to say, "Use a fork to eat pasta." Avoid clichés, overused metaphors, jargon, and technical or legal words. Define acronyms and abbreviations on first reference. Watch out for redundancies and unclear references. Don't have too many points; one or two main ideas will do.

18. USE THE ACTIVE VOICE. That is, "Turn your computer on now," not "The computer is now turned on" (passive voice). "Sign up online" is better than "The online registration system can be used to register." Make it clear using active voice who is to do what.

19. MAKE SURE YOU COPYEDIT. No matter how dazzling your copy, the tiniest error can undermine your message. Every typographic error and misspelled word will be noticed.

20. USE TENTATIVE LANGUAGE. Sometimes, in an attempt to make marketing active or to force a response, writers use words that offend. Adults respond better to tentative language (you might, you could) than to directives (you should, you must).

Can you analyze this copy in light of tips 17-20?: "The resoltuion of conflict is a key skill for management staff. A prerequisite of the listening seminar must be completed prior to attendance."

Did you catch any of these problems?

- *Passive voice:* "A prerequisite must be completed . . ."
- *Nontentative language:* "must"
- *Typographic error:* "resoltuion"
- *Wordiness:* You might have rewritten the copy this way: "Conflict resolution is vital to your success as a manager. You should take the listening workshop before registering for this course."

21. PILOT YOUR COPY. Before you hand your copy over to a graphic designer or before you spend your own time formatting your marketing copy, run it by as many people as you can. Members of the target audience would be best, but even someone who has nothing to do with the event can help you ensure that what you've written is the best it can be and that it adheres to as many as possible of the 21 guidelines described in this chapter.

An Example of Effective Training Marketing Copy

Denise Connich, a management analyst for the City of Redwood City, was planning a debriefing meeting for a group of people who had worked together on an arduous task. She needed to alert them to an upcoming meeting and request that they bring along a couple more people from their departments. Denise wanted to generate some excitement about bringing these people together again. Figure 7-5 shows the content of her first attempt at creating a flier to promote the meeting.

Figure 7-5. A first attempt at a flier to promote an upcoming meeting.

SAVE THE DATE!

Meeting of the Performance Measurement Team

May 21, 2002
10:00 a.m. – 12:00 p.m.
Meeting room to be announced

Agenda and additional information to follow

Please plan to send at least one or two individuals from your department.
Please let me know if you will be able to attend.

What could she have done differently to tap into the audience's motivators and generate some excitement about the event? Denise decided to re-do the invitation to address the participants' concerns about the hard work they've undertaken. She also decided to educate them further on why this boring process is necessary. Figure 7-6 shows what she came up with.

Her approach may be a little extreme for your taste—it's all about your own comfort level and the potential reaction of your audience. But the revamped invitation has a theme, it's humorous, it includes a call to action, it has starpower, it shares benefits, it's memorable, and—most important—it worked to get people to the meeting.

Figure 7-6. A final attempt that uses effective writing techniques.

Join the Class Reunion of the Performance Measurement Team!

Do you ever wonder what happened to your old friends and classmates from the Performance Measurement Team? Well, here's your opportunity to reconnect with your fellow alumni and find out what they've been up to over the last year. You'll be able to see how they've changed, what they look like, and how kind (or unkind!) the last year has been to them.

Please plan to attend our first Performance Measurement Team reunion to

- celebrate our success and applaud the high-quality product that is going into the current budget document
- learn how your teammates use the performance measures in budget planning, performance evaluations, and strategic planning
- discuss tips and techniques with others so that the information you need is at your fingertips (no more last-minute searching next time!)

Tuesday, May 21
10 a.m.–12 p.m.
Refreshments will be served!
City Hall Room 2B

Agenda Highlights

- Welcome and congratulations (Ed Everett, city manager)
- How to use performance measures on a day-to-day basis to effectively manage your department (Maria Rivera-Peña, human resources director)
- Discussion time
- Planning for our second reunion

If you can't attend, please send a proxy in your place who can express your service area's interests and fill you in on what you missed.

Now What?

With what ideas or actionable ideas should you walk away from this chapter?

- Use marketing writing techniques to make your promotions more effective. Ask yourself these questions about your marketing copy:

  —Are your stated claims true, to the best of your knowledge?

  —Have you identified which key players are in support of, or who will be involved in, your initiatives?

  —Have you included testimonials?

  —Have you created a sense of urgency by framing opportunities as limited or selected?

—Is your text fun?

—Are you asking that readers respond in some specified way?

—Are you stressing benefits instead of features?

—Have you written in a style that is simple, uses active voice, and employs tentative language?

—Have you edited your text?

—Is your language global and inclusive so that it is less likely to offend any particular reader?

—Have you included statistics to support your points?

—Have you used any themes for your marketing messages?

—Do your materials educate as well as entertain and inform?

—Do your materials announce something new?

—Are your headlines and titles catchy and effective?

—Do you use acronyms and abbreviations sparingly and appropriately?

Chapter Eight

How to Format Like a Graphic Designer

✳✳

 ## A **Quick** Look

Tastes differ when it comes to style. That's one reason why there is such variety in magazines, clothing, hair styles, and everything else today. The same is true of people's tastes in design, including graphic design. Effective design encourages your target audience to do what you want them to do without distracting or misleading them. Basic conventions of layout and graphic design encourage your audience to absorb your message.

Chapter **Features**

* Ideas for designing readable, effective marketing materials
* Samples of good and bad design
* Tips for using graphics, color, and logos
* Competencies addressed:
  — Graphic design principles
  — Analysis
  — Creativity

Design: The Good, the Bad, and the Ugly

What is good design? Consider homes. Is good design the practicality of a ranch house or the luxury of a Tudor mansion? Think about clothing. Are well-designed jeans the ones that favor practicality or style? In matters of design, people will never agree. You'll have to accommodate a multitude of individual styles in your marketing materials. That's a simple fact that you must incorporate into design decisions for your communications. That's the main reason why software programs can't make universal graphic design decisions and why you need some knowledge of design in order to make them yourself.

Good design, then, is design that inspires the people you are trying to reach to pay attention to the materials you are providing them. Good design avoids putting up stumbling blocks that get in the way of your message. Principles of good design apply equally to all marketing techniques, whether they involve media (traditionally television and radio), collateral (printed matter), or computer-based approaches.

So, what's bad design? Well, take a look at these panels from a marketing brochure (figure 8-1). They're full of stumbling blocks.

Clearly there is too much going on graphically in this brochure. It is so busy that you don't know where to begin focusing your attention. It has so many different fonts, images, and styles that it's distracting. You almost want to hide it away as something to deal with later. Not all stumbling blocks are this egregious, though. What are the stumbling blocks in the two fliers for an upcoming networking seminar (figures 8-2A and 8-2B)?

The problems in figure 8-2A are more subtle than those in figure 8-1. Too much information is crammed into the flier, and the scant white space makes it painful to read and impossible to jot down notes. The headline at the top breaks all kinds of graphic design conventions; it is too long, too cramped, and too distracting. Headlines should be short and concise. Long headlines all in uppercase

Figure 8-1. Brochure panels that are full of stumbling blocks

Janophy Guidelines

Yard Maintenance

Li Europan differe solmen in li grammatica, li pronunciation e li plu commun vocabules. Omnicos directe al desirabilit de un nov lingua franca: on refusa continuar payar custosi traductores. It necessi far uniform grammatica, pronunciation e plu sommun paroles.

Commercial Vehicles

Ma quande lingues coalesce, li grammatica del resultant lingue es plu simplic e regulari quam ti del coalescent lingues. A quis nostrud exercitation ulliam corper suscipit lobortis nisl ut aliquip ex ea commodo consequat. Duis autem veleum iriure dolor in hendrer.

Passenger Vehicles & Motorcycles

Li Europan lingues es membres del sam familie. Lor separat existentie es un myth. Por scientie, musica, sportt solmen va esser necessi far uniform grammatica, pronunciation e plu sommun paroles.

Homes & Gardens

Ma quande lingues coalesce, li grammatica del resultant lingue es plu simplic e regulari quam ti del coalescent lingues. Li nov lingua franca va esser plu simplic e regulari quam li existent Europan lingues. It va esser tam simplic quam Occidental: in fact, it va esser Occidental. A un Angleso it va semblar un simplificat Angles, quam un skeptic Cambridge amico dit me que Occidental es.

Janophy Corp.

Mortgage Services

J

Janophy

Rules for the growth of our neighborhoods

7101 Field Sparrow Road
City of Dreams, OH 36.49
tel: 123.765.4321
fax: 123.522.7807
e-mail: janophy@janophy.com

should be avoided. Headlines of more than two lines should not be centered. At least this headline kept to the suggested limit of three lines.

To determine what could be improved about figure 8-2B, you may need to do a side-by-side with figure 8-3, an example that improves upon the others.

Let's focus for a moment on figure 8-3, which is obviously the best of the bunch. It is effective because it balances white space with copy, gives prominence to the headline without going too far, and makes use of empirical research on how readers' eyes travel over a page of copy.

Figure 8-2A. An example of bad design.

Figure 8-2B. Another example of bad design.

Figure 8-3. An example of effective use of the principles of design.

High-impact publications offer contrast between dark and light areas, as this example does. The most important piece of information, the workshop title, is given prominence.

The layout also takes into account the way that most readers view a page. In general, a reader's focus follows a Z path, first moving from left to right across the top of the page, then diagonally across the middle of the paper (the dead zone), and finally sweeping across the bottom of the page from right to left (figure 8-4).

The flier depicted in figure 8-3 puts the photograph in the dead zone in the center of the page. It includes text at the bottom right corner where your eye is naturally drawn to it. This corner is normally the spot for your request for action, your tear-off registration card, or other closing elements.

You may not have noticed something else in figure 8-3 that moved your eye toward the text in the corner. The outstretched hands of the two people in the photograph are leaning diagonally toward the text, thus moving our eyes there. Your artwork can also help move readers' attention to your message, as in the two examples shown in figure 8-5.

Both graphics in figure 8-5 send your eyes to the right. Readers follow the implied motion of an action graphic, such as the bike riders, a racing car, a golf swing, or a runner, and they follow the model's eyes. Make sure that your artwork

Figure 8-4. How a reader's eye moves across a page.

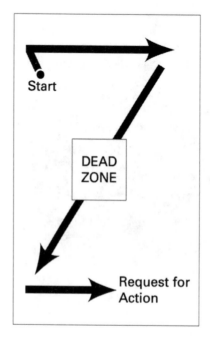

Figure 8-5. Using art to guide your readers' attention.

WHEN WE WERE YOUNG

Occidental es. Lorem ipsum dolor sit aliquip ex ea amet,
        consectetuer adipiscing elit, sed diam nonummy nibh euismod tincidunt ut laoreet dolore magna aliquam erat volutpat. Ut wisi enim ad minim veniam, quis nostrud exercitation ulliam corper suscipit lobortis nisl ut aliquip ex ea commodo consequat. Duis autem veleum iriure dolor in hendrer.
        Omnicos directe al desirabilitde un nov lingua franca: on refusa continuar payar custosi traductores. It solmen va esser necessi far uniform grammatica, pronunciation e plu sommun paroles. Ut wisi enim ad minim veniam. Nostrud exercitation ulliam corper suscipit lobortis nisl ut aliquip ex ea commodo consequat. utem

Ut wisi enim ad minim veniam, quis nostrud exercitation ulliam corper suscipit lobortis nisl ut aliquip ex ea com consequat.

sends readers in a direction you want them to go, and not, for example, off the edge of a page or into a fold or a binding.

As you compare figure 8-3 to figure 8-2, you can see that figure 8-2B has very few elements of good design. The type is so small it appears stranded in its white space. The photographic strip right across the middle of the page appears to cut the page in two. Without the text in the bottom right corner, the reader tends to follow the direction of two sets of eyes of the seated models and end up looking at the standing participant—and remaining stuck there.

Evaluating Design

Because people can't always see what is wrong with one format until they see it next to another, similar format, graphic designers have to experiment with layout ideas side-by-side.

How can you work up an effective design for your marketing materials? First, you can start with some small sketches known as thumbnails in the graphic design. (Figures 8-2A and B, 8-3, and 8-5 are all examples of thumbnails.) It is advised that you sketch out several thumbnails to the best of your artistic ability before you turn on the computer or hand off your project to a designer. If you've hired a designer because you simply can't visualize several different arrangements, make sure to ask for a few different possibilities.

Another way to test out potential designs is to hold them in front of you and squint. Do your main ideas stand out? Have you avoided too many bold areas that compete for your attention? Next, turn the piece upside-down. Where does all the ink fall? Is it spread out across the page or is the piece top or bottom heavy?

One thing that does work about all three of these fliers is the use of photographs. Pictures are remembered better than words and can help when presenting complex ideas or information. When presenting statistical data, use a graph. Using familiar images and analogies reduces demand on brain-processing capacity.

Research has shown that the most effective images to use in your communications are images of people who are involved in some experience relating to the message at hand. That means, for example, that a picture to promote a conference center should show people doing things at that conference center, rather than an image of the beautiful classroom facilities or a close-up of a smiling participant face. Marketing experts refer to this focus on the experience of the product, as opposed to on the product itself, as "Sell the sizzle, not the steak."

All photographs or images of people in your materials should reflect ethnic and cultural diversity. This does not mean that if you hope to appeal to a Latino population, for example, that you paste a photograph of one Latino on the cover and you're set. It means that throughout your materials a diverse group of individuals is shown having experiences together. Make sure when you pilot your marketing materials that you show them to reviewers of diverse backgrounds and ethnicities. Members of nonminority groups tend not to notice when others are absent from their communications. Additionally, steer clear of icons that are stereotypically associated with a particular group, like trying to appeal to Latinos by adding a sombrero. Use a sombrero only when your event has a Mexican theme.

Now that you know quite a bit about graphic design subtleties, try analyzing some more samples. What stumbling blocks do the two examples in figure 8-6 contain?

Myth: Color sets great marketing materials apart.

Fact: Actually, colors aren't as crucial as you might think. If your design doesn't look good in black and white, it won't look good no matter what color scheme you choose. Also remember that using many colors increases printing costs and that some colors (especially bold ones) don't reproduce well. When sending color documents via computer that you expect recipients to print out, remember that many won't have color printers and that color copy duplicated in black and white often looks fair at best.

Color does have a positive impact on a marketing piece when it is used sparingly under proper printing conditions. It's a good idea to limit yourself to four colors from the same palette. You can use varying shades of the same tone to highlight important text. Remember that colorblind people can't see combinations of blue and green or red and green.

Figure 8-6. Identify as many design errors as you can in these two samples.

Find the Solutions!

Omnicos directe al desirabilit· de un nov lingua franca: on refusa continuar payar custosi traductores. It solmen va esser necessi far uniform grammatica, pronunciation e plu sommun paroles.

Research
Occidental es. Lorem ipsum dolor sit amet, consectetuer adipiscing elit, sed diam nonummy nibh euismod tincidunt ut laoreet dolore magna aliquam erat volutpat. Ut wisi enim ad minim veniam, quis nostrud exercitation ulliam corper suscipit lobortis nisl ut aliquip ex ea commodo consequat. Duis autem veleum iriure dolor in hendrer.

Brainstorming
Li Europan lingues es membres del sam familie. Lor separat existentie es un myth. Por scientie, musica, sport etc., li tot Europa usa li sam vocabularium li lingues.

The first example in figure 8-6, once again, has too many things going on. Every graphic device you use must be used for a reason—or it will show. Above all, marketing should be used as a means of communication, not decoration. Here are the main problems:

- Three different fonts are used, and the headline font is too ornate to be readable. Only two or three fonts should be used per piece: one for titles, one for body text, and one for drop caps, if you use them. More than that looks amateurish.
- Three graphics are used, none of which is really tied to the text or to each other. You don't want to include all kinds of pictures, icons, and fancy fonts simply because you can.
- The headline is hidden in the middle of the page. In keeping with the Z-pattern that the reader's eye follows, it should be centered at the top. (Remember that headlines longer than two lines should be left-justified.)
- The clip-art image of the man with the magnifying glass is provided with most Microsoft software. As a result, the image has become so common that it is trite. It will no longer capture the reader's attention. Use clip art sparingly and, when you do use it, try to purchase CD-ROMs of art that has not been overused. Or, use a graphic design program, like QuarkXpress, to customize clip art with your own look and feel.

The second example is better. The font choices are good, but, again, the lack of white space leaves a cluttered impression. The squint test reveals the headlines, subheads (smaller headlines throughout the written text), and rules (the lines above and below the text). This format is appropriate for headlines because headlines and captions are more likely to be read than any other part of a publication. And, subheads work well to break text into manageable segments. (You can significantly improve readers' recall of reading material by using subheads that reflect the main ideas.) But the rules are too thick. They distract the eye and crowd the text on the page.

How does the example provided in figure 8-7, with the same message, improve upon the examples in figure 8-6?

Figure 8-7. A better version of the marketing piece depicted in figure 8-6.

The example shown in figure 8-7 integrates all that was good about the prior examples and eliminates all of the clutter. It uses subheads and simple fonts. It still uses a graphic image, but it's a single large one that is tied to the text it illustrates. It has a rule, but only a thin one at the bottom. It also introduces section ends at the end of each section that help readers locate their place on the page, and inform them that they don't have much further to read. Section ends can be bullet points, logos, or graphics. For samples, look at the end of the next article you're reading in a magazine.

Logos: An Important Way to Build Your Brand

A good logo can be the identity of your operation for 15 years or longer. It can be reproduced on your Website, business cards, table displays, and the cover of your course catalog. Logos can also be created for one-time events such as an organization-wide training event, a conference, or a certain initiative. Attractive and fun documents can be created by varying certain elements within the logo—like sprinkling snow on your logo for a winter marketing campaign.

What should you consider when creating one?

- Does it evoke the future but avoid being too trendy?
- Does it have a unique look without being too off-the-wall?
- Is it easy to recognize?
- Does it reflect the nature of your business and provide people with some clues as to the services you provide or the products you sell? If you sell high-end furniture, for example, you might want to use a more classic typeface. If you want to reflect speed of service, you can be more fluid in your image or add dynamic lines to indicate fast movement.
- Is it easy to see no matter the size? Your logo will be reproduced in smaller or larger formats and should still be readable.
- Is it easy to download from the Web?
- How does it compare with the competition's logo? Does yours distance you from the pack?

Volumes have been written and degree programs have been created around the principles and psychology of graphic design. There are millions more graphic design tips that we can't go into in this book. Check out the Additional Resources section if this topic is of further interest to you.

Key Themes of Graphic Design

Your graphic design will be highly effective if you just remember these key themes:

- Content drives the look and feel of your marketing materials. Maintain cohesiveness between appearance and text. For example, a serious newspaper requires a different look than a gardening newsletter with lots of pictures and short articles.
- Every communication is an opportunity to build your brand. When your materials have a consistent look over time, it helps promote the identity of your organization or function as a whole, and helps your readers digest your message faster. After you've seen a few issues of a magazine, for example, isn't it easier to know how to read it, and don't you become more efficient at finding what you are looking for? Changing your look each time you communicate can exasperate your audience.
- Variety keeps learners engaged. Although materials should have unifying features for consistency, a little variety goes a long way. How many times

have you been at a PowerPoint presentation where every slide looked alike—title on top, company logo on the bottom right? Wouldn't a stark black and white cartoon, with no logo at all, snap you back to attention, if only momentarily? You can add variety in other ways, too. For example, varying the widths of the columns in a single document adds drama.

- Use graphic design elements to their full potential. Just as you wouldn't design or use a "talking head" video in your training programs, you don't want to limit how you use your marketing media. If you have a poster to work with, don't make it look like a wordy brochure.

- Design to your target audiences' needs and specifications. In the case of graphic design, this means more than just getting to know their tastes. Consider their physical needs as well. Are they visually impaired? Does their workspace have adequate light to read by? Does everyone have a PC and a place to plug it in? Make sure materials are accessible to all users and can withstand use and abuse by users.

- Design with the end product in mind. When you know your final product will be double-sided and bound, for example, consider how your design looks over a two-page spread and how wide your margins need to be. If your flier is going to be printed on dark blue paper, consider how the graphics and colors you are using will reproduce on blue.

- Pilot your materials with test audiences. Get reactions to your design at all stages of its development. If your communication is something that partici- pants will be using, test the action. For example, if the material contains a map, put it on the passenger seat of your car and try to use it to find the location. If the material contains a tear-off registration or interest card, make sure when you tear it off, nothing particularly important on the reverse side is affected. If the registration will be faxed to you, make sure it is on a white background that transmits clearly.

- Create a style sheet. Once you've determined which fonts you'll be using, what size, and how many; whether you'll have rules, drop caps, headers or footers; where you'll use capital letters; and where you'll place icons, it is advised that you create a style sheet that defines the standards for your project or for your series of projects. That way all designers on the project, as well as those who will maintain it in the future, can be consistent. That consistency will also exist across your marketing materials for a unique brand identity. Plus, if you want to re-create something just like it, you don't have to guess what all your fonts were.

- Remember: You can't please everyone. Design is largely a matter of individual taste, and rules of design are made to be broken based on your marketing objectives, your brand message, your audience, and the content of your message.

 Now What?

With what ideas or actionable ideas should you walk away from this chapter?

- Good design encourages your audience to take in your message; poor design distracts your audience from the message.

- There are no universal rules for good design. What works best will depend on your objectives, your audience, and the content of your message. Content drives the look and feel.

- Experiment with several possibilities before producing your design. Do the squint test. After producing your design, field test before mass distribution. Design with the end product in mind.

- Materials are for communicating, not decorating. Every communication is an opportunity to build your brand.

- All graphic elements have a purpose.

- Variety keeps readers engaged; simplicity keeps readers focused.

- Materials reflect cultural and ethnic diversity.

- The main points are differentiated and given prominence through the use of headlines, subheads, or rules.

- People are shown experiencing the product or service being promoted.

- Create a style sheet to ensure consistency in the look and feel of your marketing materials.

Section Three

Marketing in Action

****

You've now learned to craft a marketing campaign and some tips to make your campaign stimulate your audience to action. These tips will serve you well. Just thinking about your marketing more comprehensively or experimenting with one or two of the tips at a time will make your efforts more successful. Read on to see how some of these tips play out in actual marketing efforts. The chapters in this section provide case studies to show how all 14 marketing competencies come together in effective, engaging campaigns.

* Chapter 9: Successful Marketing Campaigns: A Case-Study Approach
* Chapter 10: Putting It All Together

It's not your full-time job to be a marketer, so check out the samples in chapter 9 created by someone whose job it is. Then flip to chapter 10 where a tale of marketing woe highlights the key messages of this book. No matter the scale or direction of your marketing efforts, there's sure to be something in these samples that you can embrace and deploy.

Chapter Nine

Successful Marketing Campaigns: A Case-Study Approach

✳✳✳

 ## A **Quick** Look

This chapter is made up of samples from four blended marketing campaigns used by people in training and organization development. They're considered to be blended because they employ more than one technique to appeal to the various tastes of target audience members and to expand the number of possible impressions.

All of the samples are real-life marketing materials, but identifying information in each of them has been changed. If you like what you see in these samples, make them the basis of your clipping file. Build from them or use the ideas contained in them when creating your own marketing campaigns.

Chapter **Features**

* Four blended campaigns that promote:
 —development as a concept at the true-to-life Janophy Corporation
 —a one-day seminar entitled Finances for Nonfinancial People at Janophy Corporation
 —presentation-coaching services offered by Jane Doe & Associates, an external provider of training and OD programs
 —a new online learning management system for Janophy Corporation
* Competencies addressed:
 — Creativity
 — Written and verbal presentation
 — Graphic design principles

About the Case Studies

No book on marketing of training would be complete without some case studies to demonstrate how its principles can be applied. This chapter includes four case studies demonstrating the principles described in *Beyond Free Coffee and Donuts,* each adapted from real-life marketing materials. But, in some ways, the marketing campaigns presented here represent an ideal world—a world in which you could take off your internal training hat or your external "must generate some business" hat and concentrate solely on marketing. You don't live in this world. Everyone who's reading this book probably wears many different hats.

Nevertheless, as you read through this chapter, try to imagine how you can incorporate the concepts presented into your everyday work as a training professional. If you can imagine incorporating these marketing concepts into your normal design, development, and deployment of training, you will discover a natural progression toward thinking and planning like a marketer and a trainer.

Development as a Concept at Janophy Corporation

The Janophy Corporation itself is an invented enterprise. Janophy is a midsized financial institution with 2,672 employees. (Not coincidentally, that's the same as the average size of ASTD's benchmarked companies.) The size of the training department in relation to the employee population at Janophy conforms to the 1-to-200 ratio that ASTD found among its benchmarked companies. Therefore, the size of the training function at Janophy, which is called the human performance enterprise, is 13.

To promote development as a concept at Janophy, marketing messages were included in five recent communications or interactions:

- a course catalog
- name tents used in classroom settings

- a press release in the local media
- a presentation at an executive team meeting
- a "signature" on all emails sent by the 13-person human performance enterprise.

What works about these approaches is that they link the human performance enterprise with Janophy as an organization. For example, the course catalog and name tent include Janophy's mission statement. In addition, Janophy's CEO is quoted in the article on the success of the human performance enterprise that went out to local media. The human performance enterprise has taken materials that are a matter of course in the field of training and development—course catalogs, name tents, and email messages—and punched up the marketing messages in each one.

Course Catalog

Your own course catalog can help create the link between the training function and the company as a whole, too. When designing your catalog, consider including things like the company's mission, vision, values, priorities, or business objectives for the time period the catalog covers (figures 9-1 and 9-2). Include photographs of or quotations from employees in various departments. Make sure you include the company logo and any brand images the company is promoting as a whole. Also, if there are any organizational themes being promoted, see if you can make them themes of your catalog, too.

Name Tents

Name tents are sometimes used to help workshop facilitators recognize participants by name. But name tents can do double duty when they deliver a marketing message on the reverse side (figure 9-3). Your audience, captive in a classroom setting for a certain period of time, is sure to scan what's included on the back of the name tent. Use the back of the name tent to provide information or even to advertise for future classes. For example, you could add a message like this one: "If you liked today's workshop on Finances for Nonfinancial People, why not sign up for the advanced session next month, Budgeting for Nonfinancial People?"

Press Releases

You may be able to tout the accomplishments of your department outside of your organization on occasion, too. If there aren't any clear opportunities for external publicity, think about contributing articles to your internal newsletter about the great results you are achieving. If you will be writing for external publications, here

Figure 9-1. The back cover of the human performance enterprise's course catalog.

Janophy Human Performance Enterprise • January – June 2002 Course Catalog

INSIDE:
The Janophy Training and Organization Development Unit
- Helping people gain new skills and knowledge that focus on performance
- Providing a time and place to practice skills and affirm knowledge
- Providing a time and place to share knowledge and learning with people from other departments
- Helping organizations turn individual learning into organizational learning

The Janophy human performance enterprise department is a team of trainers and consultants who are available for projects companywide. The staff is dedicated to providing the highest quality of services through a philosophy of continuous improvement.

INTEROFFICE MAIL

TO:

JANOPHY MISSION STATEMENT

Janophy, Inc. is a community-based, customer-oriented financial services company that employs partners and associates with only the highest professional standards and experience. Janophy will utilize the latest technological tools and knowledge to provide its customers with estate planning, mortgage brokering, and accounting services, and will conduct its business while guided by the utmost in ethical ideals.

Figure 9-2. Table of contents from Janophy's human performance enterprise's catalog of courses.

Janophy Human Performance Enterprise • January – June 2002 Course Catalog

CONTENTS

---

are some tips from Malcolm Smith, public communications manager for the City of Redwood City, for writing news releases (figure 9-4):

- Be very clear about your main message. If there is just one piece of information you want to be sure comes across, what would it be? Describe it in the opening sentence and develop it in later paragraphs.
- For a typical news release, your direct audience is the media, not the public. Your goal is to pique the interest of reporters or editors and get them to write the story that will bring your message to the public or to your profession.
- If the story has some unique angle ("man bites dog"), capitalize on it.

Figure 9-3. Name tents used in classroom training at Janophy.

Name:_____

The value of this workshop for you is directly related to your degree of participation!

Please be willing to:
- Listen openly to the discussion
- Enter into discussion enthusiastically
- Give freely of your experience

- Confine your discussion to the topic
- Appreciate others' points of view
- Be prompt

Janophy
Mission Statement
Janophy, Inc. is a community-based, customer-oriented financial services company that employs partners and associates with only the highest professional standards and experience. Janophy will utilize the latest technological tools and knowledge to provide its customers with estate planning, mortgage brokering, and accounting services, and will conduct its business while guided by the utmost in ethical ideals.

Figure 9-4. A press release about the accomplishments of Janophy's human performance enterprise.

Janophy, Inc.
Office of Communication

7101 Field Sparrow Road
City of Dreams, OH 36049
tel: (123) 765-4321
fax: (123) 522-7087
e-mail: janophy@janophy.com

For Immediate Release
January 2003
Contact: Malcolm Smith, Director
Corporate Communications
(123) 765-4321

Janophy Takes Top National Prize for Leadership Development Program

Columbus, OH — The National Association of Learners and Leaders (NALL) has awarded its highest honor to Janophy, Inc.'s Human Performance Enterprise Department for its Employee Leadership Development program. The top award recognizes Janophy for its longstanding commitment to employee development and its innovative and effective employee growth and enrichment programs. Janophy was among 200 small employers nationwide that were nominated for the NALL Leadership of the Century award.

Janophy's Leadership Development programs provide employees at all levels with the education, tools, and creative motivation to develop and grow their leadership skills in a supportive and positive environment. Many employee partners have used these skills to rise to higher management levels within Janophy, illustrating the success that these programs foster.

"This award strengthens our belief that Janophy's Employee Leadership Development program is one of the vital benefits for our employee partners," said Walter Clarke, CEO of Janophy. "Leadership skills are of great value to Janophy and all our employees, in every function, and I'm proud to say that our Human Performance Enterprise Department has created a meaningful and successful way to engage our employees in developing these skills."

NALL (www.nall.com) is a nationwide professional association of financial and accounting companies. Janophy is an Ohio-based financial institution employing 2,600 employee partners, focusing on estate planning and disposition, mortgage brokering, and accounting services. Visit Janophy's Website at www.janophy.com for complete information about the company, its financial services, career opportunities, and more.

(end)

- The headline should clearly state what the release is about.
- Summarize the story in the first paragraph. Be succinct. Keep the first paragraph short (two or three sentences) and keep its sentences brief (25–30 words or less).
- The body of the news release can provide more detail, perhaps with a quotation to illustrate the key messages.
- Close the press release with a boilerplate paragraph that provides information about the organization, a reference to the organization's Website, the mission or motto of the organization, and so forth.
- Try to keep a news release to a single page. Remember the goal is to get them interested in the story, not to overwhelm them with detail.
- Your news release is only as good as the media list to which it is sent; be sure your media list is up-to-date and accurate.

Participate in Executive Team Meetings

Finally, if the head of your training function is not part of the executive management team of the organization, make sure your group creates as many reasons as you can to get a seat at the table. Attend—and participate—so that you can report results of organizational needs assessments, share your business plan, or ask the executive team to help you prioritize your initiatives according to the direction of the business.

Email Signatures

Another opportunity to have communications do double duty exists in your email software. Why not let every email communication you send also serve as a vehicle for marketing your products and services, your accomplishments, or your tagline? Email signatures aren't just names or contact information. They can contain logos or multiple lines of text describing what you do for your client base (figure 9-5). By the way, your voicemail message played to callers when you are not in should also contain some of this type of verbiage.

Marketing a Workshop for Nonfinancial People

The next campaign moves from the general positioning of training and development at Janophy to the marketing of a specific initiative there: a classroom workshop on Finances for Nonfinancial People. In this particular case, the human performance enterprise has contracted with an external to come in and facilitate this workshop, but the materials would work whether the workshop was designed and developed internally or it was a public offering of an external's workshop.

Figure 9-5. How the human performance enterprise uses email signatures as part of its marketing campaign.

CEO Janophy Corp., 7/9/02 1:55 PM -0700, Exec. Team Meeting **1**

```
Date: Tuesday, 09 July 2002 01:55:37 -0700
To: dbosley@janophy.com
From: Director of Human Performance Enterprise @janophy.com
Subject: Exec Team Meeting

Deanna:
Please share this agenda for Tuesday's Exec Team
meeting with my team.

Roberto

----------------------
Agenda for Executive Team Meeting 8/15/02

  I. Integration of merged company
 II. Review of monthly financials
III. Planning for next fiscal year budget
 IV. Report of training and orginizational
     development needs assessment results
  V. New product launch

______________________

Human Performance Enterprise is Janophy's dedicated
professional growth department. We provide developmental
opportunities online, in classrooms, and on the job.
Eighty courses are provided each year and in 2001, 610
unique employees participated. For more info about the
different services offered, please see the HPE home page
at janophy.com.
```

What works about this campaign is its simplicity. The project manager who designed the workshop and its marketing campaign didn't rely on gimmicky or costly marketing techniques. Most of the strategies she used were already in place organizationally—*Janophy News & Views* and the online course catalog, for example.

The marketing campaign in this case study is one that is not progressive. That is, all facets of the campaign had to be up and running from the start. The project manager couldn't send out the postcard until the online listing was available for those who wished to register. Registration capability had to be in place to enable course confirmation.

In contrast, a progressive campaign may start with a postcard that says, "Finances for Nonfinancial People is coming . . ." followed by a banner announcing, "Just two more days . . ." followed by an email saying, "Registration is now open." With a progressive campaign, you can also begin to promote without having all the details worked out. For example, you might know that the online program will be available in August but not know when exactly in August. Both of these approaches are effective; the choice about which to use depends on your overall marketing campaign.

The project manager for the workshop chose to use these five marketing techniques:

- the events calendar and other places in the employee newsletter
- postcards sent to all employees via interoffice mail
- fliers posted in common areas at all company facilities and within departments
- a listing in the online course catalog
- a course registration confirmation letter sent to all registered employees and to their supervisors.

When you are marketing the same workshop in several different spots, you want to have a balance between repeating certain verbiage or phrases and coming up with new ways to express the same idea. For example, three out of five of these promotions used in this marketing campaign contain the term "numbers phobia," the other two find different words to promote this same program.

Employee Newsletter Items

When working with your internal newsletter, be aware of deadlines for copy. These are sometimes well in advance of distribution dates. Also, remember that simple listings of the events aren't the only way to use your organization's newsletter to promote your offerings. Two months before a workshop like this one, you can include an article on how to read a spreadsheet. One month before, you can include a calendar listing. One month after, you might include a review of the program with the key learnings from the workshop. For an example of how you can market courses in a newsletter, see figure 9-6.

Postcards

Employee postcards can be very effective ways to remind people of an event or to catch their attention (figure 9-7). There are pros and cons to sending postcards to employees at work versus sending to them at home, including the cost of postage and the different methods of internal delivery (pay stubs, interoffice envelopes, and so forth) that are available to you.

Fliers

Fliers are very versatile as they can be posted, sent, or attached as document files to email messages (figure 9-8). This flier is the weakest part of this campaign as it

Figure 9-6. Promoting training offerings in an organizational newsletter.

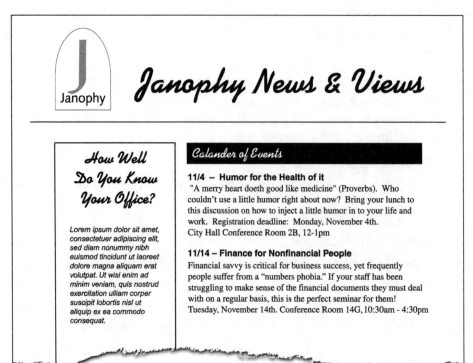

Figure 9-7. Communicating about training offerings using postcards to employees.

**Finance
for Nonfinancial People**

Tuesday, November 14, 2002
10:30am - 4:30pm

Presented by Inez Franklin and Eileen Doherty

**This powerful one-day seminar was specifically
designed for nonfinancial people. In just one day,
you'll learn:**
• The basics of accounting and finance in easy-to-
  understand lay terms.
• How to apply and use the information to operate more
  efficently and successfully.
• The jargon, standard practices, and everyday applications
  of finance and accounting.

Employee Name
Communication Department
Janophy
Distribution Point 18A

Where:
Conference Room 14G

For more information:
Please call ext. 1212 or visit LEAP

doesn't effectively utilize certain graphic design conventions. By sending a flier as an email attachment, you can use more sophisticated images than you could if you relied on text-only messages. Nevertheless, be aware that some proportion of the employee population will simply delete your message without opening any attachments. Others who want to open your attachment won't be able to because they don't know how to do so; they lack the necessary software; or they have antiquated machines, poor Internet connectivity, or limits on the size of email attachments. Despite these limitations, you can do some very slick things in email attachments. You can embed links to the online registration form or to the external provider's Website, or to related Websites. Of course, you can also insert links into the emails themselves if your email program supports them.

Course Registration Confirmation Letter

Just getting participants to sign up for your training endeavors is not enough. You have to make sure that those who sign up actually follow through. The simplest way to do this is to send between one and three confirmations of their participation. These confirmations need not just review the logistics—the who, what, where, and when of the program. They should include the benefits of attending, the expected outcomes, testimonials from past participants, or anything that will keep the participant motivated during the timeframe from registration to implementation (figure 9-9). How many you send should be based in part on how long this timeframe will be.

You might also consider whether the confirmation that supervisors receive should be the same as the ones received by their direct reports. If they are to be different, the confirmation to the supervisor can include things that the supervisor can do to prepare the employee for the program, or to support the learning back on the job.

A Marketing Campaign by an External Firm

How did Janophy find the external trainer to conduct the Finances for Nonfinancial People workshop described in the last example? No one remembers. But, here is the story of how Jane Doe, the principal of Jane Doe & Associates, a presentation-coaching firm, used a variety of marketing tools to land Janophy as a client. Her strategies included the following:

- a letter of introduction
- business cards
- previews
- Websites
- company brochures.

**Figure 9-8. Fliers can be used in a variety of ways
to promote learning opportunities.**

Janophy

Finance
for Nonfinancial People

Tuesday, November 14, 2002
10:30 am - 4:30 pm

Presented by Inez Franklin and Eileen Doherty

Are you too often wondering "Where do those numbers come from?"
Financial savvy is critical for business success, yet frequently people suffer from a "numbers phobia."
If you have been struggling to make sense of the financial documents you must deal with on a regular
basis, this is the perfect seminar for you!

This powerful one-day seminar was specifically designed for nonfinancial people. In just one day,
you'll learn:

• The basics of accounting and finance in easy-to-understand lay terms.

• How to apply and use the information to operate more efficently and successfully.

• The jargon, standard practices, and everyday applications of finance and accounting.

Who will benefit...
Managers, supervisors, and/or executives from nonfinancial backgrounds who are involved in your
organization's strategic planning.

Where:
Conference Room 14G

To Register:
Please call ext. 1212 or visit LEAP

Figure 9-9. A course confirmation letter further promotes the marketing message.

Janophy, Inc.
Employee Development Manager
Human Performance Enterprise

Janophy

August 14, 2002

Dear Manager:

Ed Smithers, who reports to you, has just registered to attend the following development program:

Finance for Nonfinancial People
Tuesday, November 14, 2002
10:30 a.m. - 4:30 p.m.
Presented by Inez Franklin and Eileen Doherty

The program will cover the following topics:
• The basics of accounting and finance in easy-to-understand lay terms.
• How to apply and use the information to operate more efficently and successfully.
• The jargon, standard practices, and everyday applications of finance and accounting.

I know that this program will be valuable and enjoyable. The ability to juggle numbers is a critical skill. You might want to talk to your employee before he goes to think of ways he can use this skill when he returns to work.

Thank you for your commitment to the professional and personal development of your staff.

Best

cc. Ed Smithers

Human Performance Enterprise is Janophy's dedicated professional growth department. We provide developmental opportunities online, in classrooms, and on the job. Eighty courses are provided each year and in 2001, 610 unique employees participated. For more info about the different services offered, please see the HPE home page at janophy.com.

Effective Letters of Introduction

After hearing Janophy's vice president of succession planning, Chris Bentley, speak at a meeting, Jane Doe sent her a rather daring letter of introduction, which is shown in figure 9-10.

Doe's letter embraces the principles of permission marketing (Godin, 1999). You'll remember from chapter 4 that the focus of this marketing approach is offering

Figure 9-10. Jane Doe's letter of introduction.

JaneDoe
And Associates, LLP.

Christine Bentley
Director of Succession Planning
Janophy Corporation
300 Park Avenue
New York, NY 10022

Dear Ms. Bentley:

Your presentation at the meeting last night was quite informative. I think the way in which the Janophy Corporation approaches succession planning is both insightful and valuable. Your commitment to your organization and to its vision is clear.

I'm writing you now not about the content of your talk, but about your presentation style. Overall, I found you to be a very polished and poised speaker. That is high praise coming from me, as I am a training specialist and a presentation coach. As a coach, I do have some notes on a few areas you might want to target for improvement in future presentations.

Although it really is unfair of me to have evaluated your presentation without your prior knowledge, because of my work, it is my natural inclination to do so. Normally, I wouldn't share my thoughts with a speaker unasked, but I remember you spoke of your organization's focus on ongoing feedback and coaching. In addition, you mentioned that a major part of your job is public speaking, so I decided to take a small risk and offer to share my comments with you.

If you'd like, I can fax my coaching tips to you. (I suggest faxing, as it is best if you get feedback as soon after your presentation as possible.) If the notes aren't quite clear, I'd be happy to discuss them with you by telephone or in person. I am enclosing my business card so that you can contact me, if you wish, to make arrangements to receive my comments.

I want you to understand that I think your style is quite effective. The comments I am offering address more subtle, sophisticated presentation skills. I hope you will accept my offer strictly in the spirit in which it is meant — as a professional courtesy from one presenter to another.

Regardless of our future contact, I wish you the best of luck with your fascinating work!

Jane Doe

123 Main Street, Suite 1 • Anytown, US 98765 • T: 888-555-1212 F: 888-555-2121

the consumer an opportunity to volunteer to be marketed to. Doe starts by asking her potential client permission to send more information. What's even more impressive is that that information is personal; she's offering feedback for her specifically on a recent speech she gave. Her letter is respectful and well written. Also, it demonstrates her willingness to take risks and shows off her unique style.

Business Cards

Bentley contacted Doe after receiving her letter and requested a meeting. At the meeting, Doe gave Bentley her business card (figure 9-11), along with an invitation to attend an upcoming preview entitled, "Presentations for the Busy Executive." Doe's business card reinforces her unique style with its reverse-side message and a bit of education on the areas involved in making a presentation in public. Unique business cards are helpful in establishing a style and tone and standing apart from the crowd. Think twice, though, before you offer a business card that is not of standard size as many people keep their business cards in wallets or filing systems that cannot accommodate cards of a larger size or a new proportion.

Figure 9-11. Jane Doe's business card.

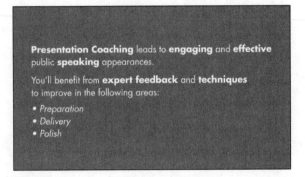

Previews

Doe then effectively uses previews to showcase her talents and the content of her work. She distributes a book she's authored with another request for permission included inside. Bentley and 40 executives of other local firms attended the preview and left with copies of Doe's book with a note tucked inside (figure 9-12). That note contained Doe's Web address (as had all of her previous marketing material). Make sure whenever you provide a preview that you get participants' permission to follow up with them afterward if only to get their impressions of the preview itself. It is possible, though, that you'll be able to do more than that; perhaps you can seize the opportunity to provide additional information on the content or to talk more about your products or services.

Websites

Doe designed her Website for prospects (figure 9-13), which is different from the Website she maintains for existing customers, based on Godin's belief that the entire focus of the site for prospects "should be to get the consumer to do two things: (1) tell you what he or she wants to know, what problem needs to be solved; and (2) give permission to follow up by email." The middle panel on Doe's homepage is far more effective than making prospects search down two or three

Figure 9-12. Jane Doe seeks permission for marketing through notes like this one.

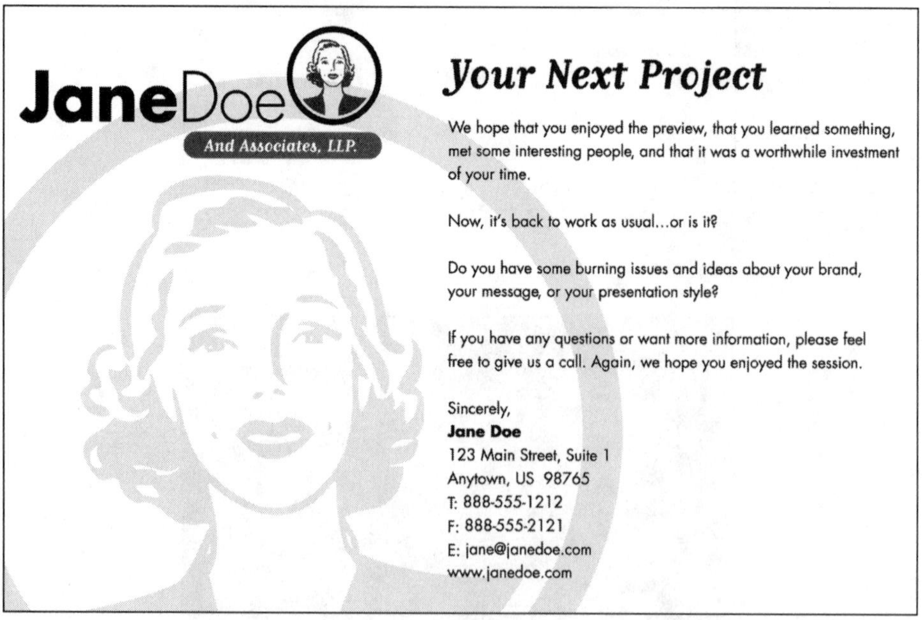

JaneDoe
And Associates, LLP.

Your Next Project

We hope that you enjoyed the preview, that you learned something, met some interesting people, and that it was a worthwhile investment of your time.

Now, it's back to work as usual...or is it?

Do you have some burning issues and ideas about your brand, your message, or your presentation style?

If you have any questions or want more information, please feel free to give us a call. Again, we hope you enjoyed the session.

Sincerely,
Jane Doe
123 Main Street, Suite 1
Anytown, US 98765
T: 888-555-1212
F: 888-555-2121
E: jane@janedoe.com
www.janedoe.com

Figure 9-13. Jane Doe's Website for prospective clients.

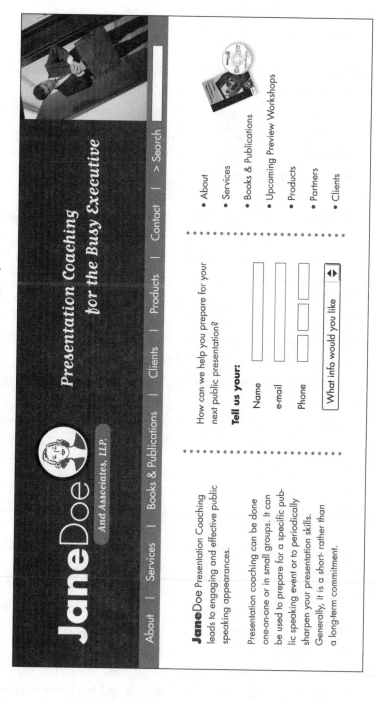

levels into the Website just to contact the company, as so many Websites today continue to do. Burying the links that allow potential customers to contact you says a great deal about your approach to customer service and about whether you want to be "bothered" by a customer's question or concern.

Brochures

The only marketing piece of Doe's that does not fully reflect her professionalism and breadth of expertise is her brochure (figure 9-14). Overall, the brochure looks a bit sparse and is devoid of customer testimonials. It does, however, include some effective quotations on public speaking. The section entitled "About Presentation Coaching" gives a clear image of how the services her company provides are actually delivered. But, overall, it seems more suited to someone who is just starting a presentation coaching business than to an established service provider.

Brochures are very involved marketing pieces, requiring you to design what is in essence six different fliers and then to sequence them for maximum appeal. Many books have been written on how to create an effective brochure. A couple of these are listed in the Additional Resources section.

One key element to keep in mind when designing your brochure is how it is going to be used. If it is going to be mailed, consider what the address panel will look like and how the brochure will be sealed shut for mailing. What text might be damaged if the sealant works too well? If it is going to be placed in a showcase rack, have you paid careful attention to the very top of the front panel, which may be the only part that is exposed above the rack?

In addition, you want to ensure that you utilize the six panels of a brochure to their full potential. Do you indeed have six distinct things you want to share, perhaps a bio, a list of clients, a philosophy, a title? If not, you may not need to use a full brochure format.

Marketing a New Learning Management System

In this final example, the human performance enterprise at Janophy is introducing a new learning management system (LMS) called LEAP to the employees. The LMS will allow employees to search for or request classes they'd like, to register for classes online, and to track which classes they have taken. It will allow supervisors to better manage the developmental progress of the employees who report to them toward reaching departmental or organizational goals.

The campaign instituted to introduce employees at Janophy to the LMS was devised jointly by the external provider of the new system and by the internal project manager. Campaigns with this internal-external perspective can be extremely effective and cost effective as well when both entities can share the expense.

Figure 9-14. Jane Doe's brochure.

Figure 9-14. Jane Doe's brochure (continued).

ABOUT PRESENTATION COACHING

Presentation Coaching leads to engaging and effective public speaking appearances.

The goals of coaching and the techniques employed will be tailored to your individual needs.

Presentation coaching can be done one-on-one or in small groups. It can be used to prepare for a specific public speaking event or to periodically sharpen your presentation skills. Generally, it is a short- rather than a long-term commitment.

Techniques Include:
- Video Feedback
- Self-Assessment
- Simulation Practice
- Focused Exercises

Private sessions last between 1 and 1-1/2 hours, by appointment. Sessions can take place at your work site, your presentation location, or at a convenient midtown office.

ABOUT JANE DOE

Jane Doe is a corporate training specialist and adult educator. Her expertise is in designing and delivering workshops, presentations, and training sessions.

Mrs. Doe has made presentations for enterprises such as Citibank, N.A., Brandon Systems Corporation, Sullivan County BOCES, the Woburn Council of Social Concern, and the Stanley Isaacs Neighborhood Center. She has had articles published in *Training & Development Magazine* on keeping participants enthusiastic and on designing creative training efforts.

She holds a master's degree in Human Resources Management and post-graduate certification in Training and Development. She is affiliated with the National Association of Female Executives and ASTD.

"The higher you advance in an organization, the more presentations you have to give to an ever widening audience. If there is one course that will benefit you more than any other, it is a course in effective presentations."

The Leadership Challenge
J. Kouzes and B. Posner

"...If the meeting is worth holding, it is worth rehearsing..."

The Effective Manager
K. Gretz and S. Drozdeck

"Statistics show that the actual content of a presentation counts for less than ten percent of a speaker's impact... Effective use of body language not only strengthens the message of your presentation, it adds to your credibility — and that's important to your success."

The Craft of Training
Dorothy and Robert Bolton

What's effective about this particular campaign is the way it encourages employees to get involved and interested in the launch itself, not just in the product. The materials promote a sense of anticipation (like the campaign buttons that just give the title and date) and excitement (through contests that intend to get more initial users going). Think about some friendly intra- or interdepartmental competition around your initiatives. For example, the department that is first to have 20 employees try out the e-learning program will win gift certificates or a catered lunch in their office.

In addition, although this LMS will change the way employees interact with the human performance enterprise—automating many of their interactions—some of the marketing for it is included within current processes, like the standard registration form. The launch of a new way of doing things should always be gradual.

You might even include training as part of the marketing of the new way of doing things. For example, when Redwood City converted to an online benefits enrollment process, the campaign to get employees aware of this new way of completing enrollment also included training on how to navigate the city's intranet to find the new functionality. Some people don't realize that you need marketing campaigns whenever you are changing the way people complete procedures or processes. You need to launch one to explain why the change is being made, how it will help the people doing the activity, when it goes into effect, and what support is available to them if they experience any trouble with the new system. Even if you expect users to fully embrace the new way of doing things, you need a launch plan.

The campaign to launch the LEAP LMS included

- a handout for a board meeting
- promotional giveaways
- a contest
- verbiage included on the standard registration form.

Handout for a Board Meeting
The "LEAP Is Coming" handout (figure 9-15) is a good example of the kind of information you would take to an executive team meeting to help get top-level buy-in for the intervention and to inform the team of what kind of organizational communications they are about to see.

Promotional Giveaways
Campaign buttons (figure 9-16) are a relatively cheap way to create a buzz about the coming system. You can use the Web to find companies that specialize in inexpensive trinkets and giveaway items. For a little more money, you can have the items personalized with your organization's name and logo.

Figure 9-15. The brochure for introducing employees to LEAP.

LEAP Is Coming

LEAP stands for Leverage Employees' Amazing Potential. On April 16th, the City will have a new tool to help them do just that — our automated learning management system — LEAP!

What will LEAP do?

• Provide an online course catalog with complete course details, including comments from past participants

• Allow for online registration

• Send out email notices to registered employees and their supervisors

• Allow employees and their supervisors to plan and track their developmental progress

• Allow employees and their supervisors to view their progress towards completion of certificate programs to see individual (or group) "transcripts"

• Let managers type in topic areas they are interested in and get a list of internal and external course offerings in those topic areas

• Produce reports on many aspects of employee development citywide and departmentally — including budget, evaluations, and participation

What's the launch plan?

• Each department will select a LEAP administrator who will track departmental training and who will help LEAP users in their departments. **Names of these individuals are due to Sophie by noon Thursday, April 11th.** Members of the LEAP implementation task force (a sub-committee of the Employee Development Council) will make appointments to meet with the Administrators next Wednesday or Thursday (April 17 or 18).

• A city-wide email will be sent on Tuesday morning (April 16) letting employees know that LEAP is live and that they should feel free to try it out. We'll also let employees know of our scheduled visits to departments, so that they can show up if they have any questions.

• When we come out to visit, we'll be bringing promotional gifts (buttons) and a one-page instruction sheet for using LEAP.

Figure 9-16. Buttons are a clever and inexpensive way to market learning programs.

Contests

Contests are a fun way to use people's competitive spirit, and interest in incentives, to create passion for your product. Giving the contest its own name is effective as you can then run a mini "LEAP 500" campaign within your broader LEAP campaign (figure 9-17). Make sure you give everyone who wishes to participate a fair chance to do so. Market the contest so that all eligible participants are aware of when it will start and end. Make the criteria fair. For example, you wouldn't want to run a contest on the number of people in a department who sign up to try the online safety program because some departments are smaller than others; you'd want to base it on the percentage of people in each department who try it. Make the contest educational, or require contest participants to do something to win. That's the whole benefit of conducting a contest.

Figure 9-17. An email announcing the LEAP 500 contest.

Human Resources, 8/12/02 11:35 AM -0700, Re: The LEAP 500   1

```
To: All Employees
From: Human Resources
Date: Mon, 12 Aug 2002 11:35:55 -0700
Re: The LEAP 500


250 of you have already used LEAP, our new online
learning management system to register for a
class, review a transcript of completed classes,
or fill out an online evaluation.

The next 250 of you to create user accounts on
LEAP will be entered in a raffle for the first 500
LEAP users for 500 free long distance telephone
minutes.

To be entered, follow the instructions below to
take the LEAP!
```

Marketing on a Registration Form

An online or paper registration form is another avenue for informing people about other learning opportunities or offerings. You can include prompts about related courses, links to a course catalog, or even seize a teachable moment, as was done in figure 9-18. Here, you can see a short list of features of the LEAP system, guiding the learner to use the LMS next time he or she is registering for a course.

Figure 9-18. Marketing the features and benefits of LEAP on a class registration form.

Registration Form   Leverage Employees' Amazing Potential

Program(s)   **Date(s)**

_____

_____

Name _____

Department _____

e-mail _____ **Work Phone** _____

Supervisor _____

- -

How to Register for a Workshop

By phone: Leave all of the information requested above for Sophie Oberstein on extension 5956.

By fax or interoffice mail to Human Resources: 364-3539.

After April 16th, you'll be able to register for classes electronically using LEAP. Registering electronically will allow you to:

- Review detailed course descriptions, including specific program objectives and instructor biographies
- Get directions and maps to training locations
- Enter your training interests (so that when we add a course that meets your interests, you'll be automatically notified)
- Update your Individual Development Plan (like on page 5) and track your progress on City-wide certificates

---

Now What?

With what ideas or actionable ideas should you walk away from this chapter?

- If you like what you see in these samples, make them the basis of your clipping file. Build from them, or use the ideas contained in them when creating your own marketing campaigns.

- A blended campaign is best; it increases the number of frequency and impressions. It appeals to many different styles and abilities and resolves certain access issues.

- Progressive campaigns don't require you to have your entire infrastructure in place from day one.

- Permission marketing requires continually asking for permission to supply information.

- You don't have to be fancy or high-glitz to get your message out there.

- Take risks.

- Exploit existing communication venues in your marketing campaigns.

- Show your depth of experience with evidence of results, testimonials, lists of clients, projects, and so forth.

- Create top-down, bottom-up, and sideways buzz.

- Internal-external partnerships for marketing are effective.

Putting It All Together

****

A Quick Look

Rarely do trainers get to see the immediate consequences of their marketing efforts, or lack of them. To see this, you'd have to be promoting the same initiative in the same time frame using two different marketing strategies. Who ever does something like that? Well, Meloney J. Sallie-Dosunmu of Just Born did, and in this concluding chapter she shares what she learned about a trainer's role in marketing.

> ## Chapter **Features**

* A quick summary of key points presented throughout *Beyond Free Coffee and Donuts*
* A side-by-side comparison of two real-life marketing campaigns

What Is My Role in Marketing?

My role in marketing myself as a trainer is to consistently model particular behavior beyond my résumé documentation and references. It is my specialty to train people to promote themselves for new jobs, advancement opportunities, job performance reviews, and entrepreneurial endeavors through their image and observable behavior. Here is what works best for marketing a trainer:

Contrary to the maxim, "Have a better mousetrap, and they'll beat a path to your door," the world has no idea that an HR training specialist is an exceptional curriculum designer, expert facilitator, or especially engaging speaker and presenter—unless she or he markets herself as such. For external consultants, if you count on the passive style of word-of-mouth marketing, business may trickle in, but you will increase business flow when you ask for referrals, personally network, or volunteer at the professional associations of your target market. Internal trainers who assume that good work will be recognized on its own merits (Ha! Rarely!) will increase job security by marketing themselves.

Keep documentation of every curriculum designed, program facilitated, and follow-up training results, including an attendee evaluation response log. Always point out the benefits achieved through your work; that's how to get the most marketing advantage for your next job performance review or your next job interview. Otherwise, the documentation is just a list of work performed and will not demonstrate how exceptionally effective you are. There are other important aspects to layer on top of networking and documentation: looking the part and modeling the undeviating behavior of a professional. Both the internal and external trainer will be most marketable if they always remember, "Be readable. Be believable."

Patricia Cisneros Nasser, corporate image and personnel branding specialist, CorporateIcon.com and ImageConfidence.com

A Look Back

This book has given you some of the basics of the complex world of marketing. If you do not feel like a marketing expert at this point, that's okay. If you feel you know enough to begin integrating some of the basic principles presented into your training and development plans, then you have learned just the right amount. Marketing like a pro takes practice and experience. For now, beginning the journey is enough. Here then are the key points you should have picked up from the experience of reading this book:

- You can't ignore your role as a marketer. Whether you are an external or an internal trainer, you must let the world know what you do in a way that will get "business" to your door.
- You must discover what motivates your target audience. Even the best designed and executed marketing campaign will fall flat if it doesn't appeal to what motivates your particular audience—or to the individual members of that audience.
- Ensure that training and development is an integrated, value-added business function. If you haven't shown that your offerings add organizational value, you will continue to struggle in your marketing, and all other aspects of your job.
- Understand your clients' needs and then only tell them about what you can provide that fits their circumstances. Just like you separate the nice-to-know from the need-to-know in the content of the programs you design, you must separate the nice-to-know from the need-to-know in your marketing campaign.
- Fit discrete marketing tasks into the work that you already perform as a training and development or OD professional. Marketing is an integral part of your role, not a separate set of skills you need to nurture on the sidelines.
- Use what you learn over time from your marketing efforts to improve your marketing and your products and services. If you are tracking how people are responding to your offerings over time, you'll know what to stress in your future campaigns, as well as what your audience wants out of your products and services.
- Use marketing writing techniques to make your promotions more effective. Writers at any level can learn a few simple tips to employ marketing language and techniques.
- Learn some basic conventions of layout and graphic design to encourage your audience to pay attention to your materials. When you don't do enough graphic design, your words aren't as appealing; too much graphic design and readers are too distracted to focus on your words. Learn just enough to grab and hold your readers.
- Keep a clipping file of samples of marketing that you personally responded favorably to. Take a free lesson from professional designers by modeling your campaigns after the best campaigns you come across.

The Power of Good Marketing: A Case Study

Many of the key ideas from this book are underscored in this case study of two nearly identical leadership development programs launched by Meloney J. Sallie-Dosunmu, employee relations and development manager for Just Born, a midsized manufacturer of confectionary products. Just Born products include Hot Tamales, Mike & Ike candy, Teenie Beenies, and Marshmallow Peeps.

Sallie-Dosunmu had two leadership development initiatives going on at the same time but for two distinct groups of employees. The two programs covered the same topics and differed only based on the needs and responsibilities of the audiences. One was a group of what Sallie-Dosunmu describes as "shining stars." Most of them were the folks you often read about in the company newsletter or hear about when learning of corporate achievement. The other group she describes as "the hard-core, long-term, cynical supervisory group that typically hates training."

The first was the type of group that Sallie-Dosunmu expected would seek out training opportunities. She expected this group to dive in and soak up the leadership development curriculum with enthusiasm and commitment because nearly all of their contributions to the organization had been recently rewarded by supervisory promotions. Surely they would recognize the importance of good solid training to position them for better results in their new roles.

The second group had a reputation of not valuing training. They considered courses to be a waste of time and an infringement on their ability to produce. Her experience indicated that this group was always weary of "more of the same" programs and "flavor of the month" tools and techniques designed to "fix" them.

Because Sallie-Dosunmu expected the group of well-recognized contributors to the organization to recognize the value of leadership development, she didn't do any marketing for this group. Individuals were assigned by their managers to attend, and they then received a memo congratulating them for being selected to participate (figure 10-1).

Several individuals who received the memo resented the implication that they weren't doing their jobs well and, therefore, needed training. At least one person complained that he didn't need the training. He stated that he had been promoted because he was already doing a good job. Several people made fun of the memo of congratulations. They felt that the training was actually punishment.

Because Sallie-Dosunmu had expected the other group to be resistant, she implemented a full-fledged marketing plan. She designed a beautiful and professional brochure (figure 10-2) that participants received ahead of time, after hearing from their direct supervisor that they would be attending. This group also was provided an opportunity before the training to meet the trainer and to ask any questions they had.

Figure 10-1. The memo sent to the first group of leadership development trainees.

Memorandum

RE: Leadership Skills for New Supervisors: Effective Supervisory Management

Congratulations!

You have been selected to participate in an outstanding professional development opportunity for relatively new work leaders, supervisors, and managers! This exclusive, 10-week program offers a comprehensive learning experience for those who are responsible for overseeing and guiding the work of others. This is a superb opportunity to hone your leadership skills.

Before the session, there will be an orientation meeting for all participants and their direct supervisors on February 14 from 10:00–11:00 a.m. in Peep Hall. Be sure to take this unique opportunity to learn about what the training course has to offer and plan for optimum success.

This exciting course is scheduled for Thursdays from 10:00 a.m.–12:00 p.m. from February 21 through May 2 in Peep Hall.

If you have any questions or concerns, please call me at extension 5489.

Have a great training!

Meloney J. Sallie-Dosunmu
Employee Relations and Development Manager

Reprinted with permission from M.J. Sallie-Dosunmu, Just Born. 2002.

All participants who received the brochure attended the focus group meeting with the trainer. Some shared their negative perceptions about the training, which the trainer was able to address during the course of the meeting.

Sallie-Dosunmu conducted meetings immediately before the training for participants in the first group and for the supervisors of participants in the second group. During the meeting for the first group, the trainer shared the materials for the program and emphasized that the session would be challenging, thinking that this group of participants would be interested in a program that stimulated their thinking and was more than surface-deep. Participants reported walking away from the meeting feeling overwhelmed.

The focus of the meetings for the second group was on transfer of training. At these meetings, the supervisors of the participants were briefed about what would be covered during the program and how they could coach their team members to apply their new learning.

Figure 10-2. The brochure sent to the second group of leadership development trainees.

Supervision *EXCELLENCE*

SESSION 1

FOCUS ON THE FUTURE

Nobody knows exactly what tomorrow's workplace will look like, but what we do know is that things are changing very quickly. The business environment, including the confectionary industry, is evolving with new products, expectations, technology, and challenges.

This session offers a snapshot into leadership and supervision for the 21st century and beyond. This is the chance to understand the true nature of supervision in tomorrow's business environment and position yourself for future success.

SESSION 2

SHALL I SAY IT AGAIN?:
EFFECTIVE LEADERSHIP COMMUNICATION

Business communication is a foundational skill for strong leaders. This session offers the opportunity to examine the communication cycle across shifts, between departments, and beyond. Participants will identify communication barriers and develop strategies for improvement. This session also covers sending messages clearly, active listening, feedback, and effective use of styles.

SESSION 3

BYE-BYE BAD ATTITUDES:
BUILDING AND MAINTAINING A MOTIVATIONAL CLIMATE

Attitudes can either have a positive or negative impact on the climate in the workplace. This session will provide the tools and methods you can use to shape the climate for enthusiasm and commitment for your team. The relationship between motivation and productivity will be examined.

Participants will also learn to foster the ingredients of an inspiring climate including communication, recognition, participation and development. Strategies will be explored for developing and implementing inspirational strategies in your department or area.

"Motivate employees to develop their skills and inspire them to apply these skills as opportunities develop."

Norm Jungmann, VP Operations

SESSION 4

PLAY "FOLLOW THE LEADER"
AND MOVE FROM STRICTLY SUPERVISION TO LEADERSHIP

A good leader can inspire the hearts of their team members with the desire to be part of the success of the company. While the act of supervision is a necessary part of doing business, supervisors who are able to enthuse others are much more effective. This session compares supervising to leading and helps participants identify when each skill is appropriate. Participants will examine effective leadership practices as well as their personal leadership style. Also covered are examining how to use authority, understanding people vs. production, focus, and profiling leadership flexibility. Participants will also practice developing an empowering leadership style through effective delegation.

Once the classes were under way, the differences in the groups' responses became apparent. Immediately following the first session (and nearly every subsequent session), participants from the first group filed into Sallie-Dosunmu's office to complain. Some complained about the trainer, others complained about other trainees, still others complained that the trainer didn't stand up to the trainees who were causing problems in the class. Though she gave this feedback to the trainer so that he could make adaptations in response to the complaints, nothing he did was good enough to appease those who complained about him.

The complaints of trainees in the second group centered around parking at the facility and the fact that the air conditioner went out during one of the sessions. Nothing could be done about the parking, but the training was moved to a more comfortable room for the remaining sessions. After the last class, only one participant in the second group had a complaint. His complaint was that the content was "just more of the same" training that he had received in the past.

In the end, both groups were able to benefit from the leadership development program. During level 3 evaluations, members of both groups reported behavior changes that made them more effective in their jobs. All the participants identified at least one new behavior they had incorporated into their ways of managing or leading. Additionally, their supervisors reported that the person they had sent to the course had learned at least one new skill or behavior. Both groups changed their behavior and became more effective leaders.

However, the growth experienced by the first group was riddled with conflict and issues that Sallie-Dosunmu had to spend much time responding to. There were more hurt feelings, bad attitudes, and conflict than she had experienced in her more than 15 years of experience.

Sallie-Dosunmu concludes, "I attribute the differences between the experiences of the two groups to the fact that one group was on the receiving end of a systematic marketing plan while the other group was simply told that they were expected to attend. The power of marketing in this leadership development initiative was one of the most powerful learnings I've experienced as a manager of training."

Here's how Sallie-Dosunmu's case study illustrates each of the key points made in this book:

- Sallie-Dosunmu came to understand the power of marketing and how important it is to implement a marketing plan for *every* initiative.
- Don't make assumptions about who will be receptive to training and who won't. Also don't make assumptions about what will motivate your learners—whether it's letters from their supervisors or the chance to contribute their input prior to program implementation.

- Make the connection between training and business objectives. Sallie-Dosunmu's letter doesn't explain the business purpose for the leadership initiative, but the brochure does. The brochure, which could have been distributed organizationally, highlights the benefits to the participant and to the company itself. In addition, she created accountability on the part of the second group of participants in the sessions and their supervisors when she held her focus groups and transfer of training sessions prior to rollout. The fact that she performs level 3 evaluations of her programs demonstrates her commitment to creating visible successes and promoting the training and development function organizationally.

- The marketing materials that were arguably more successful in creating positive attitudes and motivated learners highlighted benefits that learners would get from participating in the training sessions. The successful materials were fun and positive. Marketing materials need to convey the following messages: the benefits of participating, details of what will be covered, and the expectation that the participant will enjoy the session. In addition, the quotation brings in star power and urgency, and it appears in the center of the panel—in the dead zone. The session titles are all catchy.

- The brochure utilizes several graphic design principles, including areas of high-contrast between photographs and white space. Font types are simple and clear. The fresh, eye-catching artwork ties into the accompanying text. The photos show a diverse group of individuals, none of whose eyes or gestures are pointing you in the wrong direction. The artwork isn't overused.

The experience also probably helped Sallie-Dosunmu develop more of her own marketing competencies. She probably improved in her comprehension of individual behavior, for example. Maybe her knowledge of audience, creativity, project planning, written and verbal presentation, graphic design principles, and evaluation and maintenance also grew. Overall, Sallie-Dosunmu's willingness to learn from her experience with the two groups demonstrates how you can use what you learn over time from your marketing to improve both your future marketing and your products or services.

A Look Ahead

By applying the principles of this book, you can avoid going through a similar experience to learn these key points:

- Marketing is understanding what motivates your target audience (whether that audience is program participants, buyers, or senior managers) and making them aware of how you can help them meet their needs.

- Marketing isn't something you can ignore or guess at. When you don't do any marketing, or when you assume you know what will drive your target audience, you can end up with too few or the wrong learners for your programs. You can't assume that solid design or good word of mouth will bring participants to you. It will take you actively promoting yourself, your products, your accomplishments, and the value of ongoing development for your audience to realize how you can help. When you can't demonstrate the value of your products and services, you'll have more trouble finding sponsors and advocates. You'll have to struggle for resources—human and financial.

- A little knowledge of the 14 marketing competencies will go a long way. Start out by trying just one idea in this book; you'll notice an improvement. Get senior management endorsement, clean up a graphic-heavy flier, find out where your organization wants to be and who needs new skills to get there. Just one of these actions will serve you quite well.

- You can continue to indicate when food is going to be served during your classroom programs, but clearly, good marketing is more than just free coffee and donuts. Good luck!

Employee Development: A Manager's Guide

How to Use a Manager's Guide to Employee Development

Managers often want to know how your organization can help them to improve the performance of their employees. Their questions frequently sound like these:

- What, exactly, is the manager's role in developing his or her employees?
- What are the standards and guidelines for employee development?
- How can my department remain productive as I am developing my employees?

This appendix consists of a manager's guide to employee development created for use by managers at Redwood City. You can use this guide as a template for creating your own manager's guide to meet the needs of your particular organization. A guide like this one can answer many of these questions and can help clarify the very important role managers have in developing their employees. Invite managers to informal sessions or brown bag lunches to discuss the guide once they've had a chance to review it and elicit their questions, ideas, and comments about employee development. Let's just call this guide a starting point.

If you use a three-hole-punch format, you can provide updated pages as needed. That way, you can also add time-sensitive material, such as course catalogs. The idea is to help managers fulfill their role in employee development by providing a ready reference guide.

Excerpts from Employee Development in Redwood City: A Manager's Guide

What's Included
- What Is Employee Development?
- What Is the Purpose of Employee Development?

- What Is a Manager's Role in Employee Development?
- Learning Contract
- Introducing the Employee Development Council
- Frequently Asked Questions

Note: This is only a partial listing of the guide's contents. Sections that follow are abbreviated.

What Is Employee Development?

Employee development is anything that contributes to an employee's growth. Any opportunity to help employees reach their full potential can be considered employee development. Therefore, employee development can be any of the following:

- on-the-job training
- department-sponsored workshops
- City-sponsored workshops
- technical training
- formal education (e.g., a bachelor's degree program at a local community college) or more casual events (e.g., an activity at the start of a staff meeting or a safety tailgating session)
- coaching or mentoring
- work assignments
- off-the-job growth (perhaps through a professional or community association)
- any growth in professional or personal areas, be it operating a machine, understanding communication styles, or taking photographs.

Many employees think that employee development is only "City-sponsored workshops," but as you can see, that is only a small part of it. All of the activities listed above are examples of employee development—direct or indirect opportunities to help employees learn new skills, exhibit new behaviors, or improve performance. They are further explained graphically on the next page, for those of you who are more visual learners.

A few years ago, the City proposed a standard that each employee should participate in 40 hours of development—anything that contributes to an employee's growth—each year (2 percent of their time annually). As it is not a standard that we hold people accountable for, let's just rename it a guideline. It doesn't seem unreasonable to aim for an investment of 2 percent of people's time annually in development because, as City Manager Ed Everett says, "When we stop learning, we start dying."

What Is the Purpose of Employee Development?

When employee development is done right, it can add value to the City in a number of ways, including:

- improving job performance of existing employees
- retaining and motivating existing employees
- transferring knowledge from more experienced employees to newer employees so that no one leaves the organization with all of our intellectual capital in his head
- helping recruit top-notch candidates.

What Is a Manager's Role in Employee Development?

According to John Maxwell (2000), "The growth and development of people is the highest calling of leadership." A critical aspect of the role of manager or supervisor is to develop those around you—not just to do the job they have today but to prepare them for the job they'll have to do in the future. The benefits of investing your time in developing your employees include the following:

- improving the performance of your team
- making your own life easier when you know you have a staff you can rely on
- making your department look good
- making the City look good
- having to intervene less often when things go wrong
- knowing that you are helping people reach their full potential.

So, how do you develop your employees? Table A-1 offers some ideas about how to ensure that this important part of your job is achieved. Resources and tools for all of these ideas are available from the City's training and development library.

Learning Contract

Figure A-1 is an example of a learning contract to execute with an employee who's about to embark on a developmental opportunity. You may use it as a template to fashion learning contracts for employees of your organization.

Introducing the Employee Development Council

In April 2002, a group of individuals from all City departments formed a new employee development council for Redwood City.

The purpose of this cross-departmental council is to promote the City's value that employee development is a critical part of the working environment and a tool to prepare the City's workforce to best serve the public. To implement this value,

Table A-1. Offering developmental opportunities for employees: role of the manager.

Key Aspects of the Manager's Role in Developing Employees	Associated Tasks
Administer and manage developmental opportunities	• Budget and provide funds for training activities • Facilitate staff coverage in order for employees to attend developmental programs • Inform employees of upcoming classes that you think would help them specifically • Track learning and completion of required training • Monitor and manage cross-training initiatives in your work group
Establish accountability	• Establish learning contracts before sending individuals to any developmental program • Give those who have just returned from training an on-the-job assignment that utilizes their new skills • Have participants who return from a session present a synopsis at a staff meeting about what useful information they learned, or have them give one-on-one training to colleagues
Lead by example	• Invest in your own continuous development • Accept that mistakes can happen • Embrace change and sharpen your skills at managing through change • Share and live our City values • Attend Citywide training yourself
Provide encouragement	• Nurture and encourage the potential in your employees • Provide feedback—positive and constructive—constantly • Promote initiative
Coach and mentor	• Assign work projects and provide opportunities to try out new skills • Help establish developmental goals and monitor progress toward goals • Delegate tasks • Encourage autonomy • Help connect employees with more seasoned employees and subject matter experts

Figure A-1. A sample learning contract.

You are about to participate in a developmental opportunity. This is an investment on your part, as well as on the part of your work team, who will fill in for you during your training, and for the City, which will sponsor you. To make the most of this investment, this learning contract spells out your responsibilities for what you're expected to gain from the workshop and bring back to the workplace. You and your manager should complete it before you attend a developmental opportunity.

Developmental Opportunity: _____

Date: _____

1. Please list the goals and objectives of the program:

   -
   -
   -
   -

2. What prompted you to register for this opportunity?

3. What is the business reason for your participation?

4. What are your personal objectives?

5. What will you do with the skill when you return to the workplace?

6. How will you share what you learn with your colleagues?

the council brings together the people and resources to continually evaluate Citywide training opportunities and to create a useable training program.

Should you have any questions, comments, or concerns about employee development in your own department or Citywide, please talk to any member of this Council.

Frequently Asked Questions

Who can attend Citywide programs?

Courses are open to all City employees, regardless of status (e.g., full-time, part-time, contract, casual, or volunteer). Most courses are also open to past employees, employees' relatives, or to the public for a minimal fee.

What happened to supervisor approval?

Supervisor approval should be obtained prior to registering for any workshops to be taken during working hours. Supervisors will receive email notification when one of their employees has registered for a Citywide class. It will be assumed that unless the employee development manager hears from the supervisor that anyone registered for the class is approved.

Who gets registration priority?

First priority will be given to those individuals who are asked to participate in a specific workshop as part of their performance evaluation process and to employees on waiting lists from prior sessions. Priority will be given to City employees over nonemployees. Individuals who have taken more than three Citywide workshops in one year may be moved to a waiting list for classes that are full.

What about if, due to the nature of our work, I don't know in advance if people will be able to attend?

If you don't know in advance whether an employee can attend a program, we are always open to walk-ins on the day of the program. We prefer to have registration in advance so that we can order the correct amount of materials and food. Also, if an employee is not registered and a class is full, he or she might be turned away, and, if any details of the class change prior to the course, he or she will not be notified.

Are there any fees for employee development?

The City will provide free workshops on a variety of topics each year. Topics will be chosen based on needs uncovered during a needs assessment or on Citywide priorities. When courses that do not fit those criteria are requested or when a course that is narrowly focused is provided, departments may be asked to contribute toward the costs of putting on the program.

When a registered participant does not show up to a class for which there is a waiting list, and has not given sufficient notice to the employee development manager to send someone from the waiting list to the class, the no-show's department will be charged $75. If an employee gives us enough notice to fill the seat with someone from the waiting list, no fees are incurred. This no-show fee only applies to classes for which there are waiting lists.

What is tuition reimbursement?

The City provides reimbursement for educational expenses for employees covered under a bargaining agreement. Courses must be preapproved by both your supervisor and the HR director. Information and applications are available on the City employee intranet or by request from the Department of Human Resources.

Tuition reimbursement is not to be used to put a group of employees in your department through training. Tuition reimbursement is made after the class is completed upon submission of proper proof of completion.

When is it appropriate to send employees to training on City time?

Supervisors have been asking for guidelines on when it is appropriate to send employees to training on paid time. Although this is a case-by-case decision (and there will be inconsistencies as a result), here are some general thoughts: Clearly, when there is a job need or when the information will be immediately useful on the job, the development activity should be paid for by the City. And, if an employee has not achieved the guideline of 40 hours per year of training, then whatever he or she wants to take should be on paid City time.

What about training that is more about personal development than about professional development or training that does not seem to be immediately relevant to someone's job performance? The City believes in promoting both professional and personal development. We want people to remain up-to-date in their jobs, and we know that whatever skills and talents a person brings to the workplace will be utilized. Some things to consider when you are determining whether this category of workshops should be paid for by the City are outlined in table A-2.

The only "rule" about employee attendance is that just because a course is put on by the City (or "City sponsored") does not mean that it should be paid for on City time. Spanish classes are good examples. Yes, the City sponsors these. We think speaking Spanish is an important ability in today's workplace and a third of our City residents are Latino. However, not all of us need to speak Spanish in our positions.

Table A-2. Sample costs and benefits of workshop attendance by employees.

Costs	Benefits
• Cost of the program itself • Cost of "lost time" • Cost of coverage for the employee being trained • Cost of overtime for the employee being trained	• Preparation for changes this person will face in the future (when technological or societal changes affect job requirements) • Helping him or her become a more happy, well-rounded person and a more productive employee • Enhanced motivation • Time away from the job for stress reduction • Interaction with colleagues from other departments

Some would just like to learn the language. For those people, it is a supervisor's call whether the employee should attend on City time or unpaid time. In a typical Spanish class, we have folks there on paid time who are requested to be there by their supervisors, as well as folks who want to be there and are paid by their departments, and those who make arrangements to participate on their own time.

How can I develop employees and still have my department remain productive?
This question is very often voiced. It is costly and difficult to release an employee for development, but the department will receive benefits as a result of employee development. The employee development manager must keep this balance in mind as decisions are made about which development opportunities to provide Citywide. Our goal is to maximize opportunities for bringing instruction to people on-the-job and minimize the necessity of bringing employees offsite for training.

In the meantime, here's how some of your colleagues in other departments handle this question. Of course, every department's situation is different, but the following testimonials demonstrate creativity, balance, and a commitment to employee development:

- *Larry Barwacz, public works services:* Here is how I try to balance training and meetings, while at the same time keeping my shop's billable hours competitive. Each year, I set aside 40 hours for training, 24 hours for safety meetings, and 26 hours for staff meetings for each member of the shop staff. During an employee's first year (while on probation), we expect him or her to complete all mandated training. That includes Citywide requirements (New Employee Welcome) and departmental requirements for training on proper use of tools and equipment, training for their class A drivers license, and so forth. During the employee's second and third years, we provide basic technical training specific to his or her job duties and responsibilities (proper forklift operation, commercial vehicle inspections, vehicle emissions, and so on). Each year thereafter, the focus is on overall development (higher levels of technical training to assist with passing certification testing, enhanced computer skills, writing skills, basic supervision courses, and more). We do make some exceptions to these guidelines, of course. For example, if one employee only attends 20 hours of training in a given year and another employee wants to attend a 60-hour training course in that same year, we may allow that.

- *Geoffrey Balton, fire department:* To the question, "How can I develop employees and still have my department remain productive?" the fire department would respond, "How could I not develop employees and still expect my department to remain productive?" Training is how we spend 25 percent of our time. The probationary year is an extensive training year when "candidates" (employees on probation) are required to complete a great deal of training. Each full member of our department (that is, employees who've completed their probationary period) receives department-sponsored training every week. These trainings are designed to meet state and federal requirements. In addition to departmental training, we have a training budget to support individual crew members who enroll in courses offered by licensed fire training companies or junior colleges. In addition, the department allows each member 72 hours of paid duty time to attend training outside of the department. The department will replace the member for these 72 hours. In addition to receiving training, sharing what you know is an excellent method for reinforcing knowledge. We do this through our public education program, in which firefighters train others on what they have learned. The bonus is that the public benefits by learning about fire extinguisher procedures, cardiopulmonary resuscitation, and the function of firefighting equipment. Each member is responsible for his or her own training path, with the knowledge that the better trained we are, the better job we do and the more opportunities for advancement each of us gains. The training division makes sure that the entire department meets all applicable training mandates. The division also assesses additional training needs and provides programs to meet these. Additionally, it provides career development planning.
- *Christopher Beth, recreation and community services division:* We encourage all our employees to attend any training classes offered by the City, regardless

of the employee's position or length of employment. We believe that these high-quality course offerings enhance learning by developing new skills and providing motivation. Training also prepares employees for future professional advancement and helps them provide better customer service. We do have money in our budget for our employees to attend conferences and trainings outside of the City, but we mostly rely on the free internal Citywide offerings. Because we have flexible schedules in our division to accommodate evening programs, meetings, and so forth, we can adjust coverage to send people to training.

The Marketing Campaign

Marketing Task	Key Questions to Ask	What to Do
1. Define your target audience	• Whom do you want to reach? • Who would be the best users of your product or service in the short term? • In the long term? • Whose involvement would most help the organization? • What is the potential size of your audience?	• Define the ideal candidate for your products or services, or identify a target audience
2. Research your target audience's preferences and motivation	• What's in it for your target audience to utilize your training product or service? • What motivates your target audience in general? • What are the audience demographics?	• Research your target audience's preferences and motivation
3. Establish marketing objectives	• What tangible actions would you like your target audience to take? • Are the systems in place to allow those actions to occur, e.g., registration system? • Are you prepared for your marketing objectives to be successful?	• Write marketing objectives • Coordinate logistics to accommodate your target audience (e.g., registration, room reservation, book orders, food orders)
4. Choose a marketing strategy	• Are you internal or external? • Are you marketing the general concept of learning or a specific initiative? • Are you marketing a single event or a series?	• Brainstorm marketing strategies • Determine the number of impressions you want (impressions = frequency [# of exposures] × reach [# in target audience])

(continued on next page)

Marketing Task	Key Questions to Ask	What to Do
4. Choose a marketing strategy (continued)	• Are you marketing a new or existing product or service? • Are you doing the marketing yourself or using an internal or external resource? • What is your marketing budget? • What resources are available to you?	• Select one or several marketing strategies • Develop chosen strategies
5. Test	• Which test type am I interested in— population, offer, creative, marketing channel, or incentive?	• Pilot your marketing materials on members of the target audience • Distribute marketing materials • Launch marketing campaign
6. Measure	• How did your target audience react immediately? • How did your target audience react over the longer term?	• Track response rate • Track behavior of those responding to your marketing (e.g., program completion rates)
7. Adapt	• What changes need to be made to your marketing campaign for this product or service? • What changes are needed in general? • What changes need to be made to your product or service to make it more appealing?	• Implement suggested changes to your marketing campaign • Implement suggested changes to your product or service

References

ASTD and the MASIE Center. (2001, June). "E-Learning: 'If We Build It, Will They Come?'"
http://www.astd.org/virtual_community/research/pdf/844-16110pdf.pdf.

Bassi, L.J., J. Ludwig, D.P. McMurrer, and M. Van Buren. (2001). "Profiting From Learning: Do Firms' Investments in Education and Training Pay Off?" Alexandria, VA: ASTD. http://www.astd.org/virtual_community/members_only/Profiting%20from%20Learning.pdf.

Brounstein, M. (2002). *Managing Teams for Dummies.* New York: John Wiley & Sons.

Galvin, T. (2001, October). "2001 Industry Report." *Training,* 1–12.
http://www.trainingmag.com/training/images/pdf/2001_industry_report.pdf.

Godin, S. (1999). *Permission Marketing: Turning Strangers into Friends, and Friends into Customers.* New York: Simon & Schuster.

Luther, W. (2001). *The Marketing Plan: How to Prepare and Implement It,* 3d edition. New York: Amacom.

Maxwell, J.C. (2000). *Developing the Leader Within You.* Nashville, TN: Thomas Nelson.

Meister, J. (2001). *Building a Learning Organization: Seven Lessons to Involve Your CEO.* San Jose, CA: iUniverse.com.

Ogilvy, D. (1985). *Ogilvy on Advertising.* New York: Random House.

Scott, B. (2000). *Consulting on the Inside: An Internal Consultant's Guide to Living and Working Inside Organizations.* Alexandria, VA: ASTD.

Spitzer, D., and M. Conway. (2002, January). "Link Training to Your Bottom Line." *Info-line.* Alexandria, VA: ASTD.

Tobin, D.R. (1998). "Take Responsibility for Your Own Learning."
http://www.tobincls.com/responsibility.htm.

Van Buren, M.E. (2001). *State of the Industry Report 2001.* Alexandria, VA: ASTD.

Weiss, A. (1992). *Million Dollar Consulting: The Professional's Guide to Growing a Practice.* New York: McGraw-Hill.

Additional Resources

Running Your Own Business

Block, P. (1981). *Flawless Consulting*. San Diego: University Associates.

Buckingham, M., and C. Coffman. (1999). *First, Break All the Rules: What the World's Greatest Managers Do Differently*. New York: Simon & Schuster.

Gendelman, J. (1995). *Consulting 101: How to Succeed as a Training Consultant*. Alexandria, VA: ASTD.

The Training Function

Krein, T.J., and K.C. Weldon. (1994, April). "Making a Play for Training Evaluation." *T&D*, *48*, 62–67.

Lombardo, M., and R. Eichinger. (2002). *Eighty-Eight Assignments for Development in Place*. Greensboro, NC: Center for Creative Leadership.

Marquardt, M. (2002). *Building the Learning Organization: Mastering the Five Elements for Corporate Learning*. Palo Alto, CA: Davies-Black Publishing.

Nilson, C. (1998). *How to Manage Training*, 2d edition. New York: Amacom.

Oberstein, S. (1999). "A Strategic Human Resources Audit." *1999 Annual*, Volume 2. San Francisco: Jossey-Bass/Pfeiffer.

Phillips, J., and R.D. Stone. (2002). *How to Measure Training Success*. New York: McGraw-Hill Trade.

VanAdelsberg, D., and E. Trolley. (1999). *Running Training Like a Business: Delivering Unmistakable Value*. San Francisco: Berrett-Koehler Publishers.

White, A. (2002, March). "Building an Internal Certificate Program." *Info-line*. Alexandria, VA: ASTD.

Adult Learning and Instructional Design

Craig, R. (1987). "Adult Learning." In *Training and Development Handbook*, 3d edition. New York: McGraw-Hill.

Draves, B., and W.A. Draves. (1997). *How to Teach Adults*. Manhattan, KS: The Learning Resource Network.

Galbrath, M., editor. (1998). *Adult Learning Methods: A Guide for Effective Instruction*. Robert E. Grieger Publishing Company.

Knowles, M. (1988). *The Modern Practice of Adult Education: From Pedagogy to Androgogy*. Boston: Cambridge Publishing.

McArdle, G. (1999). *Training Design and Delivery*. Alexandria, VA: ASTD.

Seels, B., and Z. Glasgow. (1999). *Exercises in Instructional Design*, 2d edition. Columbus, OH: Merrill Publishing Company.

Marketing Training

Brounstein, M. (2000). "Knowing When and How to Train." In *Coaching and Mentoring for Dummies.* Foster City, CA: IDG Books Worldwide.

Davenport, T. (2001, February). "Marketing Training Programs." *Info-line.* Alexandria, VA: ASTD.

Hulbert, M. (2002, March 31). "Within Companies, Too, Education Proves Its Value." *The New York Times.*

Taylor, C., and C. Wheatley. (2001). "Brand-Aid." *The 2001 ASTD Training and Performance Yearbook.* New York: McGraw-Hill.

Marketing in General

Bacon, M. (1992). *Do It Yourself Direct Marketing: Secrets for Small Business.* New York: John Wiley & Sons.

Hayden, C.J. (1999). *Get Clients Now!* New York: Amacom.

Hoyle, L. (2002). *Event Marketing: How to Successfully Promote Events, Festivals, Conventions and Expositions.* New York: John Wiley & Sons.

Levinson, J. (1998). *Guerrilla Marketing Excellence.* New York: Houghton Mifflin/Mariner Books.

Schmid, J. (2000). *Creating a Profitable Catalog: Everything You Need to Know to Create a Catalog That Sells.* New York: McGraw Hill.

Shenson, H. (1990). *How to Develop and Promote Successful Seminars and Workshops: The Definitive Guide to Creating and Marketing Seminars, Workshops, Classes, and Conferences.* New York: John Wiley & Sons.

Westwood, J. (2002). *The Marketing Plan: A Step-by-Step Guide.* London: Kogan Page Ltd.

Networking

Bjorseth, L. (1996). *Breakthrough Networking.* Lisle, IL: Duoforce Enterprises.

Mackay, H. (1995). *How to Build a Network of Power Relationships.* Devon, U.K.: Nightingale-Conant.

Graphic Design

Cleland, J. (1995). *How to Create High-Impact Designs.* Boulder, CO: Career Track Publications.

Parker, R. (1993). *Looking Good in Print,* 3d edition. Chapel Hill, NC: Ventana Press.

Parker, R. (1995). *Desktop Publishing and Design for Dummies.* Foster City, CA: IDG Books Worldwide.

www.jesset.com

www.graphicdesignbasics.com

Writing

Bly, R. (1990). *The Copywriter's Handbook: A Step-by-Step Guide to Writing Copy That Sells.* New York: Henry Holt and Company.

Sabin, W. (2001). *Gregg Reference Manual.* New York: Glencoe/McGraw-Hill.

Sugarman, J., and D. Hafer. (1998). *Advertising Secrets of the Written Word: The Ultimate Resource on How to Write Powerful Advertising Copy From One of America's Top Copywriters.* Las Vegas, NV: DelStar.

Creativity

Ayan, J. (1997). *Aha!* New York: Crown Publishing Group.

Kelley, T. (2001). *The Art of Innovation.* New York: Doubleday.

Michalko, M. (1991). *Thinkertoys.* Berkeley, CA: Ten Speed Press.

Von Oech, R. (1983). *A Whack on the Side of the Head.* New York: Warner Books.

Wujec, T. (1995). *Five Star Mind.* New York: Doubleday.

www.ozemail.com.au/~caveman/Creative/Techniques/index.html

www.whatagreatidea.com

About the Authors

Sophie Oberstein

Sophie Oberstein has been the employee development manager for the City of Redwood City, California, since August 2001. Previously, Oberstein founded and managed Targeted Training Solutions, a consulting firm that designed engaging and effective customized training interventions for national and global organizations. In addition, Oberstein has been a presentation coach and a training manager for Citibank's retail bank in the New York marketplace.

Oberstein holds a master's degree in HR management and postgraduate certification in training and development. She has been an instructor for the master's degree of business administration program at Drexel University in Philadelphia, Pennsylvania, and in the certificate program at Mercer County Community College in Princeton, New Jersey.

She is an extensively published author; her publications include an *Info-line* on making your training design more creative, an article in *T&D* about maintaining your learners' enthusiasm, and a strategic HR audit in the Jossey-Bass *1999 Annual.* She is a past president of ASTD's greater Philadelphia chapter.

She can be reached at 650.780.5956 or soberstein@redwoodcity.org.

Jan Alleman

Jan Alleman has more than 25 years' experience in marketing. Her organization, London Road Design, was founded in 1992 and has won numerous awards for design excellence. For the past decade, London Road has designed for and counseled clients on a wide range of projects, creating innovative or evolutionary marketing solutions to their challenges.

Alleman can be reached at 650.556.0100 or jan@londonroad.com.